# CONCEPT-ORIENTED READING INSTRUCTION

## SOLVING PROBLEMS IN THE TEACHING OF LITERACY

Cathy Collins Block, Series Editor

# CONCEPT-ORIENTED READING INSTRUCTION

## Engaging Classrooms, Lifelong Learners

EMILY ANDERSON SWAN

*Foreword by John T. Guthrie*

THE GUILFORD PRESS
*New York   London*

© 2003 The Guilford Press
A Division of Guilford Publications, Inc.
72 Spring Street, New York, NY 10012
www.guilford.com

Printed in the United States of America

This book is printed on acid-free paper.

Last digit is print number:  9  8  7  6  5  4  3  2  1

**Library of Congress Cataloging-in-Publication Data**

Swan, Emily Anderson.
     Concept-oriented reading instruction: engaging classrooms, lifelong learners / Emily Anderson Swan; foreword by John T. Guthrie.
         p.  cm. — (Solving problems in the teaching of literacy)
     Includes bibliographical references and index.
     ISBN 1-57230-812-5 (pbk.)
     1. Reading (Elementary)—United States—Case studies.  2. Cognitive learning—United States—Case studies.  3. Motivation in education—United States—Case studies.  I. Title.  II. Series.
LB1573 .S957 2003
372.41—dc21
                                                              2002014239

*To Kent and Olivia, with love*

# About the Author

Emily Anderson Swan, PhD, is a Utah native and a Clinical Professor in the Department of Teaching and Learning at the University of Utah. A former elementary school teacher, Dr. Swan is actively involved in collaborative professional development projects with school districts and curriculum specialists, school principals, classroom teachers, and university colleagues. Her research interests include reading engagement and comprehension, curriculum integration, and creating exemplary reading instruction models. She received the Distinguished Teaching Award from the University of Utah in May 2002. She lives in Salt Lake City.

# Foreword

At the center of this book is the simple precept that engaged readers will be growing readers. Children who find that books excite them will become competent and skilled. As these children pick up books to enjoy an experience or satisfy a curiosity, they expand and enhance themselves. For them, each day brings an opportunity to engage with text on a favorite topic.

Achievement in reading is a byproduct of students' engagement. As they encounter and digest books, their competence in reading grows. Engaged readers become facile in all the cognitive systems of word recognition, sentence processing, paragraph structuring, and integrating new information with prior knowledge. Achievements and engagements are reciprocal, fueling each other for the child's benefit.

Emily Swan understands these processes. Ever since the beginning of her career as a teacher, she recognized the power of engagement. She realized early in her teaching life that children's minds draw heavily on their motivations and that achievement and affect are intertwined within each child. When a child declines in achievement, she descends in affect. If another prospers in motivation, he matures in the accomplishment of reading comprehension.

Emily Swan knows far more than the weave of these reading comprehension processes. She understands the contexts that spark and sustain them. In this book, she articulates the practices of teachers that help children become effective, engaged readers. These practices are the necessary "how-to" of teaching reading in ways that bridge multidisciplinary perspectives to support students' comprehension growth.

Beyond the how-to of reading comprehension instruction, Emily communicates the "why." She elucidates the rationale for the practices she promotes as she interweaves the research base with her intuitive understanding of how these educational contexts spur students toward reading achievement. As the text unfolds,

Emily unveils how students develop in the context in Concept-Oriented Reading Instruction (CORI).

In this writing, Emily's voice is her own. Her personal tone pervades the discourse. For those who have conversed with her, the words on the page carry her inflections, pitch, and expression. In this volume, Emily tells it as she teaches it in her classrooms. Each semester in her classes at the University of Utah, Emily conveys these ideas to her students, and often to cohorts of teachers. Through workshops in North Carolina, Atlanta, Rhode Island, and California, Emily has been reaching educators with this language. Between the lines, her urgency emerges. She was engaged in this writing, as she would have her teachers become involved in their teaching.

The pulse of this volume is a set of practices for the classroom. A dynamic network that could be termed an instructional context, these teaching actions are well documented in research. This book is grounded in principles that spring from the inquiry of educators and on empirical findings of psychologists. Its conclusions are drawn from a diverse research base, unifying previously distinct threads in its aim of assimilating the ways educators can jointly support cognitive and motivational necessities of reading. Few authors have tackled this integrative challenge so directly and so convincingly.

Some would say this volume represents the triumph of an idea. As Emily thought about the principles of Concept-Oriented Reading Instruction, she talked about them with others; presented them to teachers, seminars, and forums; and rephrased and reformed them. The expressions in this book have a simplicity that is won out of recurrence and the well-turned quality of stones smoothed in a river. This language works because it is natural in multiple respects.

Nonetheless, the language reflects its research origins. For example, phrases such as "autonomy support" have been used by motivation theorists such as Ed Deci, of the University of Rochester, to portray children's development of self-determination. However, "autonomy support" is akin to, but not identical to, teachers giving choices in the classroom. In using and illustrating such terms, Emily shows the link between research terminology and teachers' language. Her words have been fashioned to answer to a call from teachers and educational administrators, but they also reach researchers in reading.

Most impressive about this volume is its fidelity to the original language of Concept-Oriented Reading Instruction. All of the main ideas, and the terminology underlying them, are embedded here with astonishing accuracy. These constructs have been published in many research and teacher journals, as illustrated in the bibliography. A comprehensive set of key words and constructs is compiled, including the following: engagement, motivation, strategies, conceptual knowledge, social interaction, real-world interaction, autonomy support, interesting texts, collaboration support, science inquiry, and reading comprehension. Furthermore, the framework of Concept-Oriented Reading Instruction itself consists of the following: observe and personalize, search and retrieve, comprehend and integrate, and communicate to others. Each of these pivotal terms and phrases is crucial, and the uses of them are precisely sustained in this writing. There is no slippage from the original published forms of these ideas to their appearance in this novel synthesis.

It is a tribute to the author that this complex array of ideas and constructs is presented so precisely. This faithful rendering assures a link between the practices featured in this book and all of the research literature that undergirds the ideas they spring from. Hence, this volume will be a milestone as an idea and a set of practices that enable children to become the architects of their own growth in reading comprehension.

If you believe Yeats's metaphor, I encourage you to use these pages as kindling.

JOHN T. GUTHRIE, PHD
*University of Maryland*

# Preface

Concept-Oriented Reading Instruction (CORI) was developed in 1993 by Dr. John T. Guthrie and a team of elementary teachers and graduate students at the University of Maryland, College Park. Dr. Guthrie was the Co-Director of the National Reading Research Center (NRRC), shared with the University of Georgia. The NRRC had a 5-year federal grant to conduct reading research. The goal of CORI was to create lifelong learners. The original idea began with a few instructional principles for creating interest and motivation to read. These principles include social interaction; intrinsic motivations to read, such as curiosity, challenge, and involvement; and the idea of *conceptual* knowledge, building on factual, discrete kinds of knowledge. Dr. Guthrie and his colleagues knew that there were fun ways for students to become engaged, especially by learning about things in the world around them. Throwing a live frog into the picture made all of the difference. Science concepts were a natural place to start. Dr. Guthrie and his colleagues wanted to move past instruction that only had students answering the questions at the end of the science textbook chapter. They knew that for students to be *engaged*, they needed to be taught specific strategies for searching for information about a topic, comprehending this information from multiple sources and in an in-depth and thorough way, and then being able to communicate this knowledge through writing.

The CORI framework ended up coordinating nicely with Maryland's later-developed end-of-year test, called the Maryland State Performance Assessment Program (MSPAP), in which students are required to answer conceptual questions in a written explanatory format. The MSPAP serves as a model, along with programs from several other states, of how to move beyond discrete, factual kinds of knowledge questions on end-of-year tests toward the kinds of questions that require students to think and transfer reading and writing skills across content domains.

The story of how I got involved with CORI began long before 1993. After college, I began my professional life in the business world. On the side, on a volunteer basis, I taught illiterate adults to read. These adults had actually received high school diplomas without being able to read! The public school system had indeed failed them. My experience with them affected me so much that I quit my corporate job and went back to school, redirecting my path toward education. I wanted desperately to help children read while they were young so that they would not end up like my adult students, or worse.

I earned an elementary teaching certificate and taught elementary school for a couple of years. I struggled with how to motivate my students to read. When I taught fifth grade, I had one student, Christopher, who read all the time. He always had a book in his hand. He always had interesting things to talk about. He always came to school on time. He was motivated, for sure, but he was unique. Although several students in my class could read, they didn't read like Christopher. He was engaged. He *loved* to read. Other students struggled with reading, and I knew it. How could I get them to be like Christopher? How could I even get my "good readers" to *choose* to read?

In this same fifth-grade class, another student, Johnny, could not read as well as even a typical first grader. I spent the entire year marshaling help from parents and student volunteers to assist me in helping this young boy with his reading. It was my goal to teach him how to read, and we did. By the end of the year, Johnny could read and write at about a fourth-grade level. This experience changed my life, and I know it changed Johnny's life.

Through this experience, I learned that when children can read they can do anything. I also learned that if good readers have a purpose, an interest, a question to ask, they are more likely to read even more than is asked of them. I also learned that I knew absolutely nothing about how to really teach reading. I had no idea how to motivate or build competent readers. I wanted more knowledge. My question about how to motivate children to read drove me to learn more. After earning a master's degree, I was fortunate to go East.

In 1994 I began my doctoral program with Dr. Guthrie, and this is when I learned about CORI. I worked in CORI classrooms in Maryland throughout my doctoral program. During this time, Dr. Guthrie, the classroom teachers, and the graduate students continued to refine and redefine the principles underlying an engaging classroom. Once our initial CORI research ended, the CORI teachers continued teaching CORI, and I continued my research. My dissertation study investigated two CORI principles in depth, which added another principle—namely, interesting texts for instruction—to the CORI framework. Over the years new principles have been added to the framework; that is, the CORI principles continue to evolve.

This volume is based on many people's years of work. All of the CORI principles are research-based, and the research has been documented in several journal articles and book chapters. Up to this point, mostly the research aspect of CORI has been explored through publications. The CORI framework is sufficiently well established conceptually that it now needs to be shared with other teachers. Each semester that I introduce my students to these principles, they ask for this information "in a book." So, this book is for teachers and parents—or anyone who is interested in ways to engage children in learning.

Over the years I have had the opportunity of working with many exemplary teachers. One of these teachers, Margaret Barnes, is featured in this book. She has over 20 years of K–4 teaching experience. Margaret will help other teachers see how the principles of CORI "look" in a classroom. Although Margaret has only been teaching CORI for a couple of years, her instruction has always included several of the CORI principles; she is a convert. CORI is a teaching paradigm, a way of linking curriculum content and instruction in a coherent, cohesive way. When Margaret first learned about CORI in one of my University of Utah courses, her reaction was, "This is what I have been doing all along, but now I have a structure, or framework, to organize my instruction! I have direction. CORI has helped me focus on strategies and skills I want my students to acquire. It has breathed new life into my teaching." I hope the principles in this book will help *you* evaluate how *you* can create engaging classrooms that promote lifelong learners. Most likely, it will validate things you are already doing in your classroom!

I must say up front that CORI is *not* a typical reading program. There is no recipe, no teacher's manual, no end-of-chapter test, and no specified book list. CORI is not a fad, a quick fix, or a "teacher-proof" way to teach reading. CORI is not wholly teacher centered; there is no script or agenda of what to do when. There are no stickers, whistles, or bells that come with this book. CORI is a framework, a structure, for integrating curriculum with instruction. The elements are not necessarily new, but may be arranged in a way that is new to you. CORI works with what you are already teaching and is centered around your own state's core curriculum standards and objectives.

The principles of CORI are flexible. Together they create an engaging classroom, but there are a variety of ways to implement them. No two CORI classrooms are exactly alike. CORI is hard work, which is what all good teaching takes; but it is worth it, both for you and for your students. CORI is best optimized through teacher collaboration and support of the principal. So, if you are passionate about teaching and want to create a more engaging classroom, this book is for you.

# Acknowledgments

I would like to recognize the invaluable contributions of others in the writing of, production of, and inspiration for this book. First, I'd like to thank Margaret Barnes, for allowing me to share and record the CORI experience she had in her classroom. She is an exemplary teacher. Her insights and the time spent with me, both for the PBS special and the book, are so appreciated. I would also like to thank the students in Margaret's classroom, and their parents, for their willingness to participate and share their ideas, work, and classroom experiences with me.

Next, I would like to recognize the confidence, support, and patience of my editor, Chris Jennison, and all of his colleagues at The Guilford Press for their hard work and professionalism. I also appreciate the many reviewers and colleagues who read the manuscript and offered valuable feedback.

I also want to honor John Guthrie and the original CORI teachers and graduate students in Maryland with whom I was fortunate enough to work during those first years in CORI classrooms developing this framework. What a great beginning to such a fun and evolving instructional framework. It has been exciting to watch teachers' and students' lives change when they are introduced to these principles. You are my inspiration!

Finally, I am grateful to my dear family, friends, and colleagues, who have cheered me on, read the manuscript (repeatedly), offered advice, forgiven my absences, tended my daughter, fed my husband, and only asked *occasionally*, "Is it done yet?" Thank you to the incredible colleagues, classroom teachers, and students I work with in Salt Lake City and away from home. Thank you Barb and Suzy for believing in me so many years ago. Thank you Steffanie, Kati, and Jan for being my sounding boards! Thank you Mom and Dad for your amazing love and examples of diligence and consistency.

# Contents

# CHAPTER 1

## Why Is the North Pole Always Cold?

Each year is a new beginning for me. I spend hours arranging my room so that it will be a fun, comfortable, inviting place for my students. This particular year posed an additional challenge: a combination classroom of second and third graders. My classroom consists of an art corner, a reading center, a writing area, a library complete with books and large pillows, a science center, and the children's desks, which are grouped via larger tables. From day one onward, an environment of mutual respect is carefully cultivated and developed in my classroom. The children know that I think they are intelligent, important, and that they can manage their lives. We are on a journey together, to learn how to learn and to learn how to think. The children feel safe, take risks, and are engaged in learning. They are encouraged to ask questions, share with one another, and care about one another. We are a community of learners.

### WHAT IS READING ENGAGEMENT?

Reading engagement is the dynamic, recurrent process of combining motivation, strategies for reading and learning, social interaction, and knowledge about a topic (Guthrie & Anderson, 1999; Wigfield, 1997). When students in a classroom are engaged, they are learning just for the sake of learning. Their goal is to gain knowledge about something they are interested in. Engaged readers have interests and questions about the world. They are socially interactive: they want to *talk* about what they read. Sometimes, through discussion, more questions emerge; this questioning then leads to more reading, which in turn leads to more discussion. Engaged readers:

- Are active learners.
- Set goals for learning.
- Ask questions.
- Read for more information.

- Find answers.
- Gain information from others.
- Share information with others.
- Use strategies for learning.

The process of engagement is active. Concept-Oriented Reading Instruction (CORI) combines skills and strategies, knowledge, motivation, and social collaboration to build more knowledge (Guthrie & Anderson, 1999; Guthrie, Anderson, Alao, & Rinehart, 1999). This is a life-long process. For those of us who love to learn and love to read, it lasts forever. If this is so, then, why are there so many students out there struggling in school? Why do so many children think reading is boring? We know they did not begin that way.

Children are natural learners. They love to learn new things. Think how excited a child is who finally gets to go to kindergarten. These early years of school are filled with wonder and excitement. But *then* what happens? By the time students reach the fourth or fifth grade, their desire to learn has visibly diminished. School no longer excites them, and it seems for some a veritable chore to get through the day. How do we reengage their initial excitement? How do we create an enthusiasm and love for learning among our students? In the words of the Salt Lake 2002 Olympic Winter Games' theme, how do we "light the fire within"?

Many motivation researchers have been studying this question for years. We know from this research that there are three basic needs people have that motivate them intrinsically (Deci, Vallerand, Pelletier, & Ryan, 1991). This is true for everyone. *When we are intrinsically motivated, learning is its own reward.* We do things for the sake of doing them, not for something else beyond the activity.

## Competence

The first need is to feel competence. Nothing motivates people like the feeling of doing something well. When children feel capable and competent at something, such as riding a bike or playing a sport, they have fun doing it. Learning can be the same way. When students feel competent in school, they are more interested in the subjects taught, they study harder, and as a result they do better. It is a virtuous cycle. Their competence continues to increase in an upward spiral. When students feel competent, they are self-motivated. Learning is satisfying and invigorating. When students feel that they can succeed in school, they will attempt more difficult tasks, persist in the face of difficulty, and can usually summon up the effort needed to succeed. They believe in themselves—it has a very powerful effect.

On the other hand, feelings of incompetence have the opposite effect. Students who do not feel like they are capable readers, or writers, or do not know how to succeed in school, feel frustrated. Their motivation plummets. Everything seems more difficult, takes too long, is boring, and is unsatisfying. Soon these students avoid anything that appears difficult, give up easily, and eventually fall further and further behind their peers. Therefore, teaching students how to be successful learners, building their competence or their ability to be good at academic tasks, really teaches them how to be self-motivated (Deci, Vallerand, Pelletier, & Ryan, 1991).

## Autonomy Support

The second need people have is autonomy support, or choice and responsibility. People need to feel that they have choices and can do things their own way. There have been several studies showing that students whose teachers provide some choices and control over their learning became more self-motivated than the students whose teachers were in total control of what they did. Even if the choices are limited, it makes a difference. Teachers who allow their students choices about assignments, books to read, or projects, for example, increase their enthusiasm and sense of control over their learning. I discuss this principle in Chapter 5.

## Belonging

The third need that people have is the need to belong and feel that they are important to others. In school, students are self-motivated when they feel respected and accepted by others in the class. Self-motivation is fostered when teachers create a community of learners where everyone is valued and can share ideas and questions with the class. Supportive, caring teachers build on their students' interests and help them succeed in school through instruction that builds competence and fosters respect and caring relationships (Deci et al., 1991).

There are nine principles underlying CORI that create cohesive instruction and satisfy these three basic needs of all students. When these nine principles are met, students are motivated to learn (Deci et al., 1991). Margaret is one teacher who has created such a classroom. She implemented and watched her students transform themselves into self-motivated, self-directed, enthusiastic learners. Although many of these instructional principles were not new to Margaret, CORI provided the framework for these principles to be integrated in a more cohesive manner. The more excited Margaret got about her teaching, the more motivated her students became.

As Margaret concentrated on meeting these three basic needs, her students became more self-motivated. These motivations led to the use of specific strategies for learning. Margaret spent weeks teaching her students how to get the most out of the books they were reading, not only in terms of enjoying the stories but in being better able to access informational books to gain knowledge. When her selected conceptual theme was the weather, her students began reading all kinds of books about the weather. As students gained more and more knowledge about weather, their motivation increased. Their competence increased. They began sharing this knowledge with their friends. They began working with their friends to do reports and projects. Even the struggling readers and the kids who were lazy and bored got interested in the weather. Margaret first challenged them, and then they challenged themselves. Her classroom was a place where everyone could succeed. Margaret's classroom, as we shall see, illustrates how engagement in reading can be achieved from something as simple as the falling snow. Her students literally got excited about snowflakes!

## WHAT ARE THE COMPONENTS IN THE PROCESS OF ENGAGEMENT IN READING?

Figure 1.1 illustrates the four components of the engagement process. Students who are motivated to read want to gain knowledge. But, just being motivated to read may not necessarily result in gaining knowledge; students must read and then *understand* what they read before they can gain true knowledge. So, engaged readers are strategic in their thinking, and the strategies they employ lead to knowledge. Engaged readers also like to talk about what they read, so they are also social. These four components—motivations, conceptual knowledge, social interactions, and strategy use for learning—will be discussed next.

### Engaged Readers Are Motivated

Readers who are engaged in reading want to read because it is fun and interesting. The motivation to read is to learn something new or to find answers to questions about a topic and to be challenged. This kind of motivation is called *intrinsic* moti-

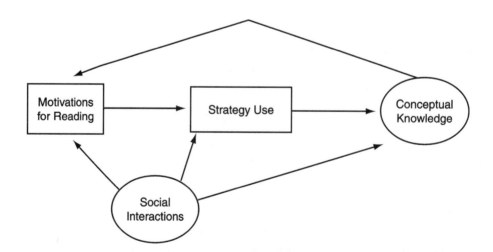

**FIGURE 1.1.** The process of engagement in reading. From Guthrie and Anderson (1999). Copyright 1999 by Teachers College Press. Reprinted by permission.

vation. When students are intrinsically motivated to read, they are reading for the sake of learning. Reading for its own sake is the goal, as opposed to some other reward. When students are motivated to read for these purposes, they become invested in and have ownership over their own learning. Motivated readers like to solve problems, ask questions, search for answers, and share the knowledge they gain with others. Motivated students are excited to read, enjoy learning new things, want to participate in school activities, put forth the effort needed to do a good job, and stick with a project until it is completed successfully (Stipek, 1996). Motivated readers are interested in the world about them. They like to learn, and often they seek opportunities to be involved in optional school projects and assignments.

Personal interest and involvement in school creates self-efficacy among students. Self-efficacy is one's own belief about one's ability to accomplish a task (Bandura, 1986, 1993). In this case, it is one's own belief about the ability to read and to learn. Self-efficacy is powerful and influences the student's choices of activities. The choices that students make also affect their ability to persist in the face of difficulty, how much effort they will put into a project or assignment, and how well they will accomplish their task. Self-efficacy also influences how well students learn and apply new information. Students who are self-efficacious must evaluate how much they already know, based on their background knowledge or previous experiences, and how this knowledge will help them incorporate new information or new skills (Schunk, 1984). When students have low self-efficacy, they see reading and new learning as difficult tasks. These students are not fully able to think about what they already know and how it can be applied to a new situation or to new knowledge. When self-efficacy is low, learning is compromised. When teachers, however, are able to foster and build students' self-efficacy, they increase students' ability to learn. Research has shown that instructional processes can positively influence and increase students' self-efficacy and intrinsic motivation to learn (Guthrie & Cox, 1998; Guthrie et al., 1999, 2000).

## Engaged Readers Seek Conceptual Knowledge

There are many levels of knowledge. Content knowledge is a type of knowledge about the physical, social, or mental world. One can have knowledge about planets, animals, and cultures. Within content knowledge is domain and topic knowledge. For example, within the content of animals could be the domain of reptiles, and a topic within reptiles could be turtles. Topic and domain knowledge work together (Alexander, Schallert, & Hare, 1991).

In most learning situations, both domain knowledge and learning strategies are important. Knowledge must go beyond facts that are static and linear (such as in the television game show *Jeopardy*). The highest levels of learning include knowledge in the form of concepts that are dynamic and that integrate basic facts, relational understandings, and principles within a domain (Alexander & Judy,

1988). So, if students are studying turtles, they learn the various *facts* about turtles, such as their physical characteristics or features. In addition, students learn about the *functions* of these physical features. When students understand how the features of turtles function, they can apply these functions to other species of turtles in the water and on land, comparing and contrasting how turtles live. Building on this knowledge, students can then learn about the *systems* of turtles, such as their life cycles, food chain relationships, adaptations, habitats, and survival tactics. This is *conceptual* knowledge—the relational and systemic understanding of a topic or subject matter. Conceptual knowledge represents a deep level of processing that builds systemic or relational understanding. When students gain this deep level of understanding, they are able to problem solve and then to transfer information within a particular domain; for example, the habitat of one reptile may be similar to the habitat of another reptile, and that may have implications for both species. According to Alexander, Schallert, and Hare (1991), students have gained conceptual knowledge when they are able to develop higher-order principles that explain the relationships and factual information they have read.

Gaining information about nearly any domain and about the world in general is done primarily through reading. Engaged students continually build on their background knowledge and extend it through reading and learning new information. When students read informational texts, they extend their knowledge by searching for the "big picture" or "main principles" at the center of the domain. As students gain knowledge through reading, they also become better able to apply this knowledge to solve problems or to answer questions. This knowledge is often transferable to other types of reading materials, as well as other areas of their life. In narrative texts, students use their knowledge to solve problems related to the plot, characters, and theme. The knowledge gained in reading helps students to understand the "main theme" or "conflict and resolution" in a book.

Research suggests that students gain conceptual knowledge when five conditions exist. The following model by Glynn (1994; Glynn & Duit, 1995) is based on an extensive review of this research:

- Existing knowledge is activated.
- New information and experiences are related to existing knowledge.
- Intrinsic motivation is developed.
- New knowledge is built.
- New knowledge is applied, evaluated, and revised.

## Engaged Readers Are Social

When students are engaged, they talk about what they are reading. Have you ever read a book based on someone's recommendation? The concept of book clubs is not new, but think of the purpose of them: it is to discuss books. Whether sharing ideas from books in a fourth-grade classroom or reading one of Oprah's Book Club books, people everywhere love to talk about what they are reading. Talking about what we read is fun and motivating; it connects us to one another. There are numerous benefits to being a reader, many of which are social. Frequent and active readers are more involved in the community. Active readers vote, join civic and community organizations, and are more likely to participate in parent–teacher associations and to be members of religious groups (Guthrie & Anderson, 1999; Guthrie, Schafer, & Hutchinson, 1991). Active readers are informed, involved, and connected to other members in the community because they share a common information base. Engaged readers are socially interactive. They share knowledge and resources. Social interaction about reading leads to increased amounts of reading (Guthrie, Schafer, Wang, & Afflerbach, 1995); it also increases achievement in reading (Wentzel, 1996). Chapter 7 focuses on the social aspects of reading in the classroom in greater detail.

## Engaged Readers Use Strategies for Learning

Lastly, engaged readers develop strategies to access and understand texts of all kinds. Engaged readers have cognitive strategies for making decisions, processing and retaining information, making sense of text, organizing their time, and setting goals. Reading is an active, conscious process. Students need cognitive strategies to be successful. Likewise, teachers need instructional procedures for helping their students become successful and motivated to learn. When students learn how to learn, they are thereby able to gain in-depth conceptual knowledge.

Engaged readers reflect upon their prior knowledge, since in order to fully digest new understanding one's prior knowledge and experience must be evaluated. When students refer to their own background knowledge about a topic, the new information found the text is easier to understand and apply. Research shows that readers' prior knowledge about a topic helps them to make inferences and increases their comprehension of the text (Dole, Duffy, Roehler, & Pearson, 1991). Text is therefore normally more difficult to understand without some requisite background knowledge. Teachers can help students to activate their own background knowledge through modeling or thinking aloud, prereading questioning, small-group discussions, and brainstorming (Dole et al., 1991).

Engaged readers monitor their comprehension and ask questions. When students monitor their understanding, they are aware of when the text is confusing or does not make sense. When meaning breaks down, engaged readers know how to remedy this problem through "fix-up" strategies. Monitoring comprehension is crucial to gaining in-depth knowledge. Questioning leads to deeper levels of comprehension and helps students organize their thinking (Williamson, 1996). Questioning also creates a purpose for reading. The more one reads and understands, the more motivated a reader one becomes. Gaining conceptual knowledge is motivating, which leads to social interaction, continued strategy use, and then this knowledge base is increased. This is how the cycle of engagement is both recurrent and dynamic. Each element builds upon the next, creating engaged, active learners.

## WHAT DO ENGAGED READERS LOOK LIKE?

Margaret's second- and third-grade students are studying the concept of weather. On a cold January day in Utah, her students were outside watching snowflakes fall from the sky. You might be wondering, who has time to do this? Everyone, at least in Utah, has seen snowflakes before. What is the big deal? But Margaret's students were definitely *engaged*.

In Margaret's class the students are studying weather for a whole semester. This is not a 10-day unit on the seasons and different kinds of weather. Weather may seem like a commonplace occurrence, but these students are thinking about weather in a whole new light. The are *really studying* it, and they are not in a hurry. Margaret's students will spend weeks on everything about weather: tornadoes, hurricanes, weather patterns, weather cycles, predicting weather, clouds, rain, sleet, hail, snow, heat, and how weather affects plants, animals, and the seasons.

Before the students observed the snowflakes, several events took place that led up to their intense sense of engagement. Margaret had a purpose. Let's examine what she did to create such excitement about something as simple as snowflakes.

> We began the year by studying life cycles. We spent the first part of the year learning about butterflies and other metamorphic animals. We read books, kept journals, raised butterflies from pupae, wrote reports, shared information with other classrooms, wrote poems, stories, and did a lot of art.
>
> After the holidays, we moved to biographies. The children were eager to choose a person and learn everything they could about that person. However, we all began together by reading the biography of Helen Keller. We all had copies of the book, and we read and discussed the book a chapter at a time. We recorded our responses in journals. We wrote a class report together about the life of Helen Keller. We talked about important elements that should be included in a report. I did lots of modeling. The kids got plenty of practice.
>
> As a closure to the biography unit, I read the book *Snowflake Bentley*. The children were amazed at the photographs of snow crystals. They loved the book, and we read it several times. Each time we read it, they came up with new questions.
>
> "How did he make his camera?"
> "Why did he want to take pictures of snowflakes?"
> "How long did he take pictures?"
>
> This turned out to be a wonderful introduction to our study of the weather. Through the use of this book a seemingly ordinary weather phenomenon became an exciting event.

Early on during the weather unit, Margaret provided the opportunity for students to ask their own questions about the weather. Again, you might be thinking, how hard is asking a question? But in many classrooms teachers are the ones who invariably ask the questions. At other times, students might answer questions that are in the back of the chapter. Seldom do students' questions serve as the starting point or focal point for learning; but, in Margaret's classroom, importantly, *they do*.

Margaret shared several books with her students to generate interest in various topics closely related to weather. As Margaret read, she began to ask herself questions aloud. She would say, "I wonder what causes snowflakes to form?" Then, as she read, students began to ask questions too.

"How come they are all different?"
"How can so many snowflakes be different?"

The students' questions continued. Margaret continued to read as the students continued to think about what she was reading. This led to a wonderful discussion about snowflakes that lasted long after she had finished reading the story.

*Snowflake Bentley* was the first hook. The students were fascinated by his interest in weather. We read the book *On the Same Day in March* and had quite a discussion about the fact that different parts of the world are experiencing different kinds of weather on the same day. We pulled out the globe and charted on the globe the different kinds of weather that various regions of the world would have on that particular day. That prompted the students to begin asking questions."

"Why is the weather different?"
"What happens at different times of the year?"
"Are there places where the weather never changes?"
"Why is the North Pole always cold?"
"How does weather affect the animals in the different countries?"

Thus began the students' initial interest in the weather. We decided as a class that we would become weather watchers. We even took notebooks outside to draw pictures of the current weather. We started charting and graphing the weather conditions and the temperature. It was a perfect place to begin. It was early January in Utah: *winter!*

As the class monitored the changing winter temperatures and the cloud formations and cold fronts, Margaret had the students think about things they wondered about in regard to the weather. The students wrote their questions on sentence strips, signed their name at the bottom, and taped the strips up on the board in the front of the classroom. The students asked such questions as: Why does the weather change? What causes tornadoes? What causes hurricanes? Why does it get so cold in the winter and so hot in the summer? Why are there seasons? The questions went on and on.

At any time students could add questions that came to mind as they thought and learned about the weather. Soon Margaret would teach them *how to ask* good questions, but not on this day. This day was for students to just think and wonder about the weather.

As snowflakes began to fall outside one day, Margaret noticed her students looking out the windows more than usual. She heard more conversations among the kids about the books they had been reading and about snowflakes during the remainder of the day. By day's end, she hoped the snow would keep falling for a few more days.

This is the beginning of engagement! The key to keeping engaged readers talking, searching, questioning, and reading more is an opportunity to learn about something broad and concrete—such as the weather—in a new way.

Throughout this volume, you will see how Margaret finds ways to help her students gain knowledge about snowflakes and other aspects of the weather through her teaching. The students want to find interesting books and resources to answer *their* questions, and she is happy to help them find answers. Margaret will show them how to search for information, gather and synthesize it, take notes, and figure out strategies for holding and recording their thinking. Finding answers is exciting for engaged readers; they want to share this knowledge with others. Margaret will help them find ways to share their knowledge with others in meaningful ways. Essentially Margaret is teaching her students how to *learn*. Once her students know how to find information to answer their questions about snowflakes, they will also know how to find information about tornadoes. And that is how this dynamic, recurrent process unfolds and repeats itself. This is engaged reading. Engaged reading is the result of coherent, well-planned instruction. As you can see, there are several things Margaret does in her classroom that create links between reading, writing, and the weather. Her instruction is both goal-oriented and cohesive.

## WHAT DOES AN ENGAGING CLASSROOM LOOK LIKE?

The difference between a classroom where students are engaged and one where they are not consists in the teacher's instruction. This whole volume is about instructional principles that, once implemented, can create engagement. When teachers follow these principles and incorporate them into their daily routines, the entire classroom is engaged, including the teacher. The key to long-term success is building coherence throughout the days and weeks of each term.

### Coherent versus Fragmented Instruction

What do I mean by coherent instruction? Coherent instruction is teaching that helps students make connections throughout their day. Coherent instruction connects reading with writing with spelling and the use of the English language. Reading and writing, in turn, connect to science, social studies, and math. These content areas, in turn, connect to students' interests and questions, which are at the motivational hub for genuine learning.

When instruction is coherent, teachers show students how to use techniques to comprehend a variety of texts. Through instruction students learn that cognitive strategies are readily transferable across content areas. Learning becomes easier because the same skills and strategies used to comprehend a novel also are of help in understanding issues of war or how to create a story problem in math.

When students can read well they:

- Make connections to their own lives.
- Determine what is important.
- Synthesize information.
- Visualize what is happening in the text.
- Understand enough to explain or retell what was communicated.

Once students realize this power, their interests can be fed, their questions can be answered, and knowledge can be gained on any topic. School becomes more fun because students begin to perceive the connection between reading, writing, and content areas. Students thereby become engaged readers.

Coherent instruction cultivates student engagement because reading engagement is a process of connecting. Students are more likely to stay engaged when they have time to find interesting books, when they are able to develop the skills and strategies to be better readers, and when they can talk about what they are reading with their friends. These conversations go beyond the classroom. Soon students choose to read on their own time. Reading becomes social as they share books and interesting facts with their friends, which creates new discussions about books and learning. These conversations lead to knowledge gaining and sharing, which in turn motivates more reading and learning.

Everywhere I go, teachers tell me that if they could change one thing about their day it would be to have *more time*. A classroom where the teacher helps her students make these links themselves, building on their own prior knowledge and interests, is a classroom where instruction is coherent and where students are engaged. When reading, writing, and content are combined, there is more time to teach concepts in greater depth. The day is spent reading and learning about several important topics. This type of instruction makes much more sense than what we typically see in elementary classrooms, namely, *fragmented* instruction.

The opposite of coherent instruction is fragmented or compartmentalized instruction. When I used to teach elementary school, I had "compartmentalized" teaching segments. School began at 8:30, and I spent the first 30 minutes taking roll, listening to announcements, answering questions, and orienting students to the day's schedule. A typical day looked like this: reading from 9:00 to 9:45, spelling from 9:45 to 10:00, recess from 10:00 to 10:15, language from 10:15 to 10:45, math from 10:45 to 11:30, lunch from 11:30 to 12:15. Then, in the afternoon I had silent reading from 12:15 to 12:30, science from 12:30 to 1:15, physical education from 1:15 to 2:15, social studies from 2:15 to 2:45, and then students finished projects, turned in assignments, and cleaned up until the 3:00 dismissal bell rang. Once a week we had time in the library. A few times a week we alternated phys ed with art and health. Needless to say, I never felt like I had time to teach anything *thoroughly*. Does this sound familiar?

This kind of schedule was the way I was taught to teach. Everyone in the school taught this way. We had different books for reading, spelling, and language, as well as for silent reading. Seldom did one teaching segment connect to another. In fact, when I taught fifth grade, our school divided our students into ability groups for reading and math. So, I did not have all of my own students for these subjects. Another year, grade-level teachers decided to "specialize" in a content area. This way, one teacher taught the science for all the fifth graders for a semester, and another teacher taught the social studies for the next semester. As teachers, our rationale was to make things easier for us. Things were easier on us in terms of content, but this method of instruction only created more distraction for the students. My instruction was completely fragmented; it was the opposite of coherent instruction.

Every semester I try to build the case for all my students, both preservice and in-service teachers, that they need to teach literacy skills all day long. For many students of mine, some of whom have been teaching for several years, this is quite a paradigm shift. I know—I went through the same shift. I visit several classrooms during a semester. Rarely, however, do I find teachers showing students how to bridge reading strategies across content areas. Oftentimes, teachers may have taught their students excellent comprehension strategies with novels and stories but fail to revisit them when it comes time to read a book chapter about the Battle of Gettysburg, or the emancipation of slaves. I ask them, "How do students learn about the U.S. Civil War without *reading* about it?" The concept makes sense to all of them, but how can they do it? They tell me, "We simply do not have *time*."

Over the years I have found that teachers just need to be taught how to show their students how to transfer reading skills from one subject to another, or from one type of reading material to another. I had to be taught, too; the concept was once new to me. But it makes sense. Once I saw CORI classrooms in action, I realized how powerful Concept-Oriented Reading Instruction really is—not only for the students but also for the teacher. The CORI teachers I work with seem to have so much more *time to teach*. This precious commodity seems to increase when students are highly engaged and when teachers integrate curriculum and make their instruction more cohesive (I will discuss teacher involvement further in Chapter 7). Many of you are CORI teachers in terms of your philosophy about teaching, but you may not yet have assembled all the pieces. Coherent instruction is based upon nine principles, which are listed at the periphery of Figure 1.2. These nine principles include learning and knowledge goals, real-world interactions, interesting texts, autonomy support, strategy instruction, collaboration support, teacher involvement, evaluation for engagement, and rewards and praise. Each of these nine principles will be discussed in more detail in subsequent chapters.

## Creating Coherence in Your Classroom

In the next seven chapters you will learn how to incorporate and weave these nine principles into your classroom. Most of these principles will be familiar to you, and many of them you may already have in place. As you read, think of how you like to teach and what you are willing to give up, add, or change to help your students become more engaged and to meet their three basic needs: a sense of competence, autonomy support, and belonging. CORI principles can be adapted to any grade level and used with any type of content. For ease of illustration, the examples in this volume are in the life sciences and earth science, but social studies concepts are just as easily adaptable as well. Hopefully, by the end of this particular text, you will have a Concept-Oriented Reading Instruction teaching framework that will enable you to enhance your own teaching.

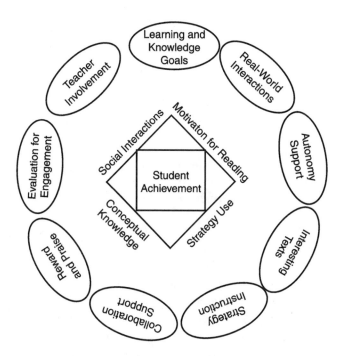

**FIGURE 1.2.** Nine principles of coherent instruction. Adapted from Guthrie et al. (2000). Copyright 2000 by The Guilford Press. Adapted by permission.

# CHAPTER 2

## What's Your Goal?

The first principle of coherent instruction is having a *purpose* for learning. Many researchers consider goals for learning to be the same as motivations for learning (Meece et al., 1988; Wentzel, 1996). When students are motivated to learn, they quickly develop a plan. When students set their own goals for learning, amazing things can happen. When the degree of accountability and personal investment increases, students take an active role in learning. Goals affect both students and teachers. If teachers do not have a purpose for what they want their students to learn, and a plan to carry out this purpose, how can we expect our students to be engaged and invested in school? Purpose is everything!

### PRINCIPLE 1 OF COHERENT INSTRUCTION: LEARNING AND KNOWLEDGE GOALS

### What Are Learning and Knowledge Goals?

Goals are defined here as reasons, or purposes, for learning about concepts in science, social studies, and other content areas. The goals of learning and knowledge refer to core learning goals that teachers develop *with* their students while also complying with state core curriculum standards. When teachers' goals for students are about *understanding the concepts* more than just "getting the right answer," students are more likely to believe that they can do the hard work of gaining knowledge. Students whose goals are to learn are more likely than other students to be more engaged, to use cognitive strategies, and to link their new knowledge to previous knowledge (Meece, Blumenfeld, & Hoyle, 1988). Students with learning goals choose learning tasks that are challenging. These students are concerned with their own progress—they *want* to learn. Learning or knowledge goals are goals that improve one's level of competence or understanding. Learning is valued as an end in itself. Students with learning goals tend to choose activities or learning tasks that are *interesting* to them, even if they do not initially feel competent to deal with the material (Meece & Miller, 1999).

On the other hand, students whose goals are solely to do better than others or to show off their competence through competition are often less "engaged" in learning (Meece et al., 1988). That is so because their goal is less a matter of gaining knowledge than it is outperforming peers, getting a better grade, or receiving other kinds of rewards. When students' goals are not knowledge-driven, the focus is on the reward rather than on the knowledge itself. I will discuss rewards at greater length in Chapter 8.

## What Do Learning Goals Look Like in a Classroom?

Teachers can create learning goals by using long-term conceptual themes to organize instruction. If reading comprehension is valued for its own sake, it becomes a learning goal; if, instead, it is valued for points, stickers, or pizza parties, it no longer is a learning goal (Guthrie, Cox, et al., 1998). Research has found strong links between goals and academic performance. Meece and Miller (1999) found that when students' focus is on learning goals, they are more likely to:

- Prefer and choose challenging tasks.
- Persist at difficult tasks.
- Seek forms of help that promote independent problem solving.
- Use cognitive strategies that enhance conceptual understanding.

Oftentimes in school we hear complaints from students that they are bored. This usually means one of two things: (1) we are not challenging them enough, or (2) they do not understand what they are reading or doing, or the task at hand. When we teach students "how to learn," their competence in reading increases, as does also their motivation.

My first goal was to get that group of students who struggled with reading, and lacked confidence in themselves as readers, to be successful. I also wanted to help the students who either didn't care about school or were too lazy to put forth the effort necessary to be successful. I wanted them to learn that they could do it. I had a lot of books on a lower reading level, so even the most struggling reader could find weather-related information. I had books with incredible photographs of lightning storms that were so fascinating that no one could resist them. My goal was to have everyone learning about the weather, regardless of where they started. I didn't want anyone left out!

A second goal was to teach my students how to ask good questions. I knew that if they could ask good questions it would motivate them to find a lot of information to answer the questions. We spent a lot of time talking about questions. I really had them think about what it was that they were interested or curious about. They got really good at questions. This questioning strategy really mushroomed because the students learned what each other asked; everyone's questions were posted in the front of the room. They talked to one another about what they were finding. The students who were all studying lightning exchanged sources, or resources. Once they learned how to dig deeply for information, they got really excited and just kept asking more and more questions.

A third goal for my weather unit was to teach my students to seek several sources for information. I wanted them to go beyond just looking in the encyclopedia, almanac, or the more traditional repositories of information. One of the ways I accomplished this was to have a vast "library" of books for my students about the weather. Another way was to get my students to think of resources that they could find on their own. One day we brainstormed about this and they came up with several sources: parents, newspapers, experts such as the weatherman at the local television station, the Internet, reference books, trade books, and their own personal observations about the weather. Their ideas helped me to better assess what strategies they needed. I tried to shape my strategy instruction around the idea of helping them be resourceful. This worked out nicely, being the most natural route, as well. When we went to the computer lab to search for information, for example, I taught the students how to submit a word or phrase for a web search. We found really fun websites about the weather and storms. The kids loved it. It was fun to teach them a new skill because, when we tried it, a vast array of information came up on the web. I was learning too, and so it was genuinely exciting for me. The Internet adds a whole new dimension to learning from now on.

A fourth goal was that I wanted to move beyond one end-of-the-unit report. I wanted the students to see that learning is a continuous lifelong process. I wanted to teach them, in an indirect way, that we don't just learn about the weather for 4 weeks and then we're done. We can read more and more and more and learn things forever; it doesn't have to end. I wanted them basically to see that if they can get excited about learning, they can learn about anything they want. Once they have the tools to access information, gather it, organize it, and make sense out of it, they can do this over and over again. That actually happened with this unit. My students wanted to do report after report after report. They talked about the weather nonstop. They really loved the process of learning. It was the best feeling to see them get it! They learned all that from studying the weather! Who could have known?

Research suggests that students who are focused solely on performance goals do not process information as deeply but rather do the minimum required to outperform others. This often translates into copying word-for-word out of the book, various memorization and rehearsal strategies, and an emphasis on finishing the test or project "first."

Judith Meece and Samuel Miller (1999) conducted a longitudinal study in North Carolina in grades 3, 4, and 5. There were two cohorts of students in the study. The first cohort consisted of 203 students in grades 3, 4, and 5. The second group included 228 students in grades 3 and 4. Questionnaires were given to the students to assess their goal orientations. Their various goal orientations were observed over the ensuing school year. Learning (or task) orientation questions included such ones as:

- "I really wanted to understand the assignments."
- "I wanted to do better on this assignment than I have done before."
- "I wanted to learn as much as possible."

The performance goal orientation questions included:

- "I wanted others to think I was smart."
- "I wanted to do better than other students."
- "I wanted to get a good grade on this assignment."

The third category of questions included questions about work-avoidance goal orientations. Work avoidance is a negative motivation to read or work. Students with work-avoidance goals tend to exert the *least* amount of effort required. Questions about work avoidance included:

- "I wish I didn't have to do this assignment."
- "I just wanted to do what I was supposed to do on this assignment and get it done."
- "I wanted to do as little as possible."

The results of the study were interesting in terms of goals. For all grade levels, learning and performance goals *both* decreased during the year. Interestingly, for each grade level—3, 4, and 5—students claimed to have "learning" as their goal more than "performance." By the end of the year, however, both of these goals had decreased for students in all grade levels. So, not only did they care less about learning, they cared less about outperforming their peers. The greatest differences came in the work-avoidance goals.

All of the third graders' goals (learning, performance, and work avoidance) decreased over the year. In the fourth and fifth grades, however, the work-avoidance goal *increased* during the year for both boys and girls. Boys, however, were more likely than girls to have work avoidance as a conscious goal.

The results of this initial study raised questions for the researchers about what the teachers were doing in terms of their instruction. Meece and Miller (1999) were interested in the teachers' classroom instruction and the role it played in learning, performance, or work-avoidance goals. So, the researchers examined classroom instruction to see how it affected students' goals. An intervention study was conducted with 187 children in grades 3, 4, and 5, as well as eight teachers. The researchers looked at the assignments the teachers gave their students. The assignments were divided into two categories: simple and complex.

Simple assignments included independent skills, factual recall, teacher control, and short answers. Complex assignments, on the other hand, included social collaboration, lengthy exams, the opportunity to study over time, reading multiple paragraphs of text, and many writing assignments. Teachers were encouraged to decrease the simple assignments over the year. Not every teacher did this in the same way. Four of the eight teachers implemented these changes in their classrooms, meaning they used fewer "simple assignments." These four teachers were three to four times more likely to use complex assignments than were the other four teachers.

Meece and Miller (1999) found that students who worked together collaboratively, had multiple reading and writing assignments, and could work on projects over time cared less about outperforming others over the course of the year. Moreover, students at every achievement level—high, medium, or low—in these "complex assignment" classrooms were less likely than their classmates in the "simple assignment" classrooms to state that their goals were performance-based. These students said that they did not care about trying to outdo others or to be better than others. One more surprising result was that students who were typically "low" achievers did better in the classrooms with the complex assignments than in the classrooms with the simple assignments. So, what does this important study tell us? It tells us that goals make a difference, both for the teacher and her instruction as well as for her students.

## How Do I Implement Learning Goals in My Classroom?

Classrooms that promote a *combination* of intrinsic and extrinsic motivations in complex reading and writing tasks can influence students' goals. For example, grades are a reality in school; but, the emphasis does not have to be *only* about the grade itself or *which* students are getting the *most* points in a contest to get the *best* grade. When getting an "A" or winning a contest is the teacher's goal for her students, then the students' goals are also about performance more than learning. The problem with most contests for points is that someone has to lose; nobody likes to lose. Learning may or may not happen in these cases. On the other hand, fostering students' *intrinsic* curiosity, challenging students' thinking, or having students work together in small teams to accomplish a common goal, should be emphasized *more than* the grade itself. Students who are intrinsically motivated are more engaged in deep learning and they also end up getting the "A."

In addition, the *ways* in which teachers connect curriculum to instruction can influence students' goals for learning. Teaching a concept on a worksheet with limited answer choices, where students work independently, is not as exciting as if students get to interact with a phenomenon, ask their own questions about it, and then find answers in fun books. Teachers should do more to provide opportunities for student input and choice, more closely link instructional activities to students' interests, promote interactions among students of different achievement levels, and allow for multiple opportunities to complete challenging academic tasks and assignments. These complex assignments create more engagement. Students will still have to be graded; but grades are an afterthought, not the goal. There is no need for a contest when only certain students win, because everyone can win—meaning everyone can learn. *Learning* is the goal.

> One of my favorite aspects of CORI is that my students became so self-motivated. They wanted to work on their weather unit all day long! They would ask me, "Can I keep this book at my desk?" "Can we stay in for recess? Do we have to go outside?" As soon as they finished one project they immediately wanted to study another topic. Once they were done with tornadoes, they wanted to study floods. They wanted to study about everything!
>
> The students began to realize that the weather affected everything in their world. They became so much more observant about how weather changed everything around them. They were fascinated by everything. They started to notice evergreen trees and why they don't lose their needles. They realized how weather affected plants and how people's lawns and gardens changed in the winter. They wanted to know how and why the snow built up on the chain-link fence. They went outside and just watched the snow and the design it made on the chain-link fence. Normal everyday things we take for granted were fascinating to them. It was the most fun I have ever had teaching!

Engagement is created when students have opportunities to rely on their intrinsic motivations such as curiosity, challenge, involvement, and self-efficacy, or their belief that they are competent readers. The teacher's job is to create a classroom where learning is the goal. When learning is the goal, students are more likely to employ wiser cognitive strategies, talk with their friends about their knowledge, be self-directed, make choices that keep them challenged, and have fun learning.

According to Deborah Stipek (1996), to foster students' learning goals teachers should incorporate the following guidelines into their classroom practices:

- Provide numerous opportunities to demonstrate mastery, through students' sharing of their knowledge with others (I will deal with this in greater detail in Chapter 7).
- Adapt instruction to your students' knowledge, understanding, and personal experience.
- Provide opportunities for discovery and experimentation.
- Success should be defined in terms of improvement. Effort, learning, and

working hard should be emphasized rather than getting a precisely "right" answer or outperforming others.

- Mistakes should be treated as natural and normal steps in the learning process.

These beneficial classroom practices lead to positive student beliefs about themselves as learners, which eventually lead to more favorable student outcomes. When students believe they are competent, have control over their scholastic outcomes, and they attribute poor outcomes to low effort or ineffective strategies and good outcomes to effort and ability, then they are likely to be successful in many ways. Stipek (1996) observed that these classroom practices encourage students to have goals, to master tasks, to develop skills, and to learn. These goals result in students' being intensely involved in tasks and learning. Students will choose challenging tasks, take risks, and persist when things get difficult. They will also use effective strategies to solve problems and to monitor their progress. Learning will be at a conceptual level, and students will feel self-respect and satisfaction when they achieve success.

## Concept-Oriented Reading Instruction Is Learning-Goal Oriented

Margaret had several goals for her students, among them:

- To help struggling and unmotivated readers enjoy reading.
- To teach students how to question the world around them.
- To teach students how to be resourceful and adept at finding information.
- To build a collaborative community of learners.
- To teach students to love learning.

In Margaret's classroom the primary curriculum goal of her instruction was for the students to learn about the weather. Everything she did in science and literacy connected back to her weather theme. Margaret supported students' individual goals for learning by encouraging them to ask their own questions, to collaborate socially, and to choose their own activities, topics, and projects. The easiest way to promote learning in your classroom is to follow the nine CORI principles. When writing an instructional plan, the easiest place to begin is with your goals.

## BUILDING A CORI UNIT

### Choosing a Conceptual Theme

The first step in building a CORI unit is choosing a conceptual theme. "Conceptual themes" differ from "thematic units" in several ways. A kindergarten teacher in Pennsylvania gave me a perfect example of a thematic unit: apples. She has her students draw apples, eat different kinds of apples—golden delicious, granny smith, mackintosh—and then categorize them. They read a story about Johnny Appleseed. They learn how to make applesauce. They make caramel apples. The dot-to-dot math worksheet forms an apple. They do math problems using pictures of apples. For rewards, the students get apple stickers. This unit lasts for about 3 weeks. This thematic unit, however, is *not* a conceptual theme.

Conceptual themes are broad subject matter ideas in science, social studies, history, music, and other areas. In elementary school the content areas that are easiest to integrate with reading are science and social studies, but you may choose to integrate any content area. To explain how to choose a conceptual theme, I will use science and social studies topics here because they are the most commonly used. These themes are based on overarching concepts that may even combine several topics within the same content area. For example, in science the conceptual theme of weather combines the topics of water, air, and the seasons. These are three required science topics for third graders in Utah. Conceptual themes are sufficiently broad that teachers can focus on each concept for 16 to 18 weeks. Other conceptual units in science may include various animal species' adaptations, habitats, life cycles, growth patterns and systems in the human body, as well as land forms, the earth, energy, and the solar system. Social studies themes may include war, discrimination, cultures, countries around the world, America, Utah (i.e., your own state as a theme), prejudice, heroes, and power. There are as many ideas for conceptual themes as there are fertile minds.

## Implement Your State Core Curriculum

The first step in choosing a conceptual theme is to look at your states' core curriculum standards and the specific requirements for your grade level in reading, or the language arts *and* in science (or any other content area you choose to integrate).

Second, list the major content area topics you are required to cover during the year in science or social studies—for example, for third grade science, plants, animals, water, weather, rocks, and minerals. CORI integrates either science with reading or social studies with reading, but not both at once. CORI is not designed to integrate all six subjects you teach, although I have seen teachers integrate science and reading and bring math concepts in when it is appropriate.

Third, list the major language arts or reading strategies you are required to cover during the year. Reading is something we do all day, but we read about many topics and in many different types of text. Your goals in teaching reading should be to teach your students not only how to "learn to read" but also how to "read to learn." This involves strategy instruction in both decoding and parsing unknown words, vocabulary development, and several comprehension strategies. These reading strategies are specifically outlined in the "Search and Retrieve" and the "Comprehend and Integrate" phases of CORI (discussed in Chapters 4 and 5, respectively).

## Create a Conceptual Theme Timeline

A conceptual theme should be broad enough to cover the regular grading period in your district or school, which generally vary from 12 weeks to 18 weeks of instruction. Here are some options:

1. *Semesters.* If your school's grading period is based on quarters, each one is about 9 weeks long. Rather than teach four 9-week units, combine two quarters into one semester. This way you would have two semesters and could teach two units for 18 weeks each. You'll need to divide your curriculum into two broad conceptual themes.
2. *Trimesters.* If your school's grading period is on trimesters, they are about 12 weeks long; so, plan three units of 12 weeks each.
3. *Entire year.* If you have one very broad theme (such as animals or the weather), you may decide to cover it for the entire year.

Once you have the "timeline" for your unit, you need to decide what conceptual theme to teach. Combine similar topics to make fewer, but broader, themes. You should have one theme for each semester or trimester. For example, you might combine the weather topics for the third grade into the following themes:

- *Semester themes*: Unit 1—How weather affects plants and animals; unit 2—How weather affects rocks and minerals.
- *Trimester themes:* Unit 1—Weather; unit 2—Plants and animals; unit 3 —Rocks and minerals.
- *Entire year theme:* Weather.

# CHAPTER 3

## What Interests You?

Finding a way to meet the individual needs of your students begins when you can find topics that interest them. Although pedagogically it seems impossible for all 30 students in your classroom to study completely different things, with CORI it *is* possible. Once a broad conceptual theme is chosen, there are numerous interesting topics that students can study. But, first, interest must be created. In this chapter we will explain Principle 2 of coherent instruction, namely, real-world interactions.

### PRINCIPLE 2 OF COHERENT INSTRUCTION: REAL-WORLD INTERACTIONS

#### What Are Real-World Interactions?

Real-world interactions consists in looking at, touching, feeling, tasting, smelling, and listening—that is, really experiencing—an object or phenomenon. Observations also consist in interacting with this object or idea. Real-world interactions also include data collection, data analysis, and experimentation, especially if the conceptual theme is science-related. Real-world interactions can take many forms. There is a continuum of interactions from the abstract to the concrete. The more *concrete* the experience is, the more *powerful* it is. We can all probably remember when we were young and made snowflakes by folding paper in special ways and then cutting various designs with scissors. Opening up the folded paper was always exciting when our cutwork design was revealed. Think how powerful making snowflakes could be when combined with factual knowledge about snowflakes. An important activity that Margaret included to create interest in the weather was the study of snowflakes. Spending time observing real snowflakes in the making added to students' understanding of the weather in a new and exciting way.

One week in January the weather had been very snowy. The students had measured the snowfall each morning at the weather station and had recorded it on the weather chart and in their journals. One day, Margaret noticed that the falling snowflakes were especially large and soft.

I looked out the window and noticed that the flakes were *huge*, and it made me think about *Snowflake Bentley.* I said to the kids, "Look at the snow-flakes—aren't they big?" All of a sudden, everyone ran to the window to look at the snowflakes. They were large and soft, and the kids wanted to look at them up close. I decided it might be a good idea to go outside and observe them firsthand. I asked the students if they wanted to go outside and do an experiment with the snowflakes. The kids said, "Yes! Can we go right now?" So we put on our coats, hats, mittens, and boots and walked down the hall. Someone from another class asked us where we were going. Chase said with enthusiasm, "Out to watch the snowflakes!" Boy, did we get strange looks! When we got outside, the kids watched the flakes fall on their coats and on their sleeves. One person took off her mitten, and the snowflake melted instantly in her hand. Then someone asked, "How did Snowflake Bentley catch the snowflakes and look at them before they melted? Our hands are too warm; they melt the snow-flake too fast. What did he catch them with?"

The students were so curious about how Snowflake Bentley caught the snowflakes long enough to look at them. We needed something cold. So I ran down to the faculty room and put some construction paper in the freezer. We had read in *Snowflake Bentley* that the shape of snowflakes depended on the temperature outside and how much moisture was in the air when it snowed. We also learned that the amount of pollution in the air could affect the crystals' ap-pearance in interesting ways. So, we decided to try an experiment with the cold, colored paper to see if we could keep the snowflakes frozen long enough to ex-amine them closely with a magnifying glass.

The students decided to have me put black paper and blue paper in the freezer because the kids thought it would be easier to see white snowflakes on dark paper. While I went and froze the paper for a few minutes, someone went back into the classroom and got the box of magnifying glasses out of my cup-board. After about 10 minutes, I got the cold paper out of the freezer, and ev-eryone tried the experiment to see if the cold paper could keep the snowflakes from melting. It was a blast!

The kids noticed that the snowflakes were huge. From reading *Snowflake Bentley* they remembered that snowflakes change with weather conditions. So, since these were huge snowflakes, the students deduced that there must be a lot of moisture in the air and the temperature must be really cold. Every student was engaged! They were catching snowflakes on their tongues, checking the temperature at the weather station, and taking notes [see Figure 3.1]. Some stu-dents found that certain magnifying glasses worked better than others. The kids could have stayed outside all day [see Figure 3.2]!

This firsthand experience got us so excited about snowflakes, when we got back to the room, that we immediately reached for our copy of *Snowflake Bentley* and looked through it again. There was another book with the actual

**FIGURE 3.1.** Nathan discovers a new and exciting way to catch snowflakes!

**FIGURE 3.2.** Students examine snowflakes with their magnifying glasses.

photographs of snowflakes that Wilson Bentley had taken with his camera. I was able to find this book at the library and brought it to school. The students pored over this book, looking at real photographs of snowflakes. They also found his website!

This observational activity was so exciting for the students because they actually got to apply what they had learned from *Snowflake Bentley* to their own lives. Observing the snowflakes and looking at them with the magnifying glasses set the scene for more questions and validation of what they already knew about snowflakes, climate, and how crystals form. The exciting part about this observation was that it fascinated the children for weeks. The students all wrote about this experience in their journals. Margaret took pictures of the kids observing the snowflakes. Then she displayed them on a poster, along with a class-written journal entry of their fun day (see Figure 3.3). Real-world interactions are most memorable when several senses are used to observe and interact with the objects. Learning in this way can leave a lasting impression.

Observing snowflakes falling, seeing them magnified, and doing experiments with them on cold construction paper represents the ultimate in engaging educational experiences. Short of that, seeing a video about snowflakes is normally more compelling than a photograph of one, which in turn is more instructive than a diagram or drawing of a snowflake, which finally is still more substantive than just hearing a description of a snowflake.

If you live in San Diego, observing snowflakes can be problematic, so real-world experience must take another form. Be creative. Think of ways that teaching would be fun for you. If you are having fun, your students will too. The closer to "real" the experience is, the easier it is for students to become interested and connected.

Students can interact with all kinds of objects and even animals to teach concepts, depending on your conceptual theme. One example might be real-life adaptations during the life cycle. In the fifth grade students sometimes observed hermit crabs to learn these concepts.

The concept of the life cycle and growth is made more interesting when students get to interact with real hermit crabs. Generally students place the animals in clear plastic containers and aquariums and interact them in the classroom, learning about their habitat, how they grow, how they survive, and how they adapt to their environment. Interacting with live animals firsthand creates a situation where students ask questions, with these questions in turn leading to a desire to learn more about the animals. This initial interest in hermit crabs leads to curiosity, which is intrinsically motivating. Soon, students take the idea of the life cycle of a hermit crab and extrapolate it to other animals. They are engaged. Students may have some prior knowledge of hermit crabs. They may have seen pictures of them, read about them in a book, or been told how strange they look. But holding one and keeping it in a container on one's desk to observe is quite different. Students now have the opportunity to really study hermit crabs closely.

**FIGURE 3.3.** Margaret's class wrote a collaborative journal entry to remember the fun they had observing snowflakes.

Students interact with hermit crabs by looking at them on their desks, watching them walk sideways, and catching them before they scurry away. The feel of the hermit crab's legs in cupped hands is ticklish and thrilling. There is excitement in telling your friends that you held one. Seeing their beady little eyes up close is a new experience. The way they retract into their shells is new. All of a sudden, hermit crabs seem much more interesting when they are in your hand than you thought they would be by just looking at a picture of one.

A few weeks after the snowflake experience, several classes in our school got to go on a field trip downtown to see the Olympic ice skating trials at the Delta Center. Since Salt Lake was to play host to the 2002 Olympic Winter Games, this was an exciting opportunity for the kids. Before the performance began, we had to wait outside for our entire group to assemble. It started to snow! What luck! The kids began to notice the snowflakes landing on their coat sleeves. They were so excited! The snowflakes were huge! They knew that the crystals were bigger because the air was colder and there was more moisture in the air. They were running around like crazy trying to get the kids from the other classrooms to join in their excitement. Snow is so commonplace in Utah, however, that the other kids weren't interested. They didn't have the same interest, excitement, or enthusiasm that my kids did. But, then again, they did not have the knowledge about snowflakes, climate, humidity, pollution, or crystal formation that my class had. They just wanted to get in out of the cold. When it came time to go inside, my class didn't want to go because they were so caught up in their snowflake observations.

The thing that made this episode so exciting to me as a teacher was the fact that it wasn't just one or two students who were excited about the event—rather, the entire class was caught up in the discovery. In my 20 years of teaching I don't ever recall having that level of interest generated in any other project we were working on. The students could hardly wait to get back to school to record their observations in their weather journals.

Although Margaret could not affect the weather, she used it to teach concepts. The information about snowflakes incorporated concepts about temperature, moisture in the air, and the formation of crystals. Helping students make these connections with real-world interactions and books made all the difference for these students. They were able to see the relationships among these concepts about weather and superimpose this new knowledge onto their own background knowledge about snow.

## What Do Real-World Interactions Look Like in the Classroom?

Real-world interactions can take several forms over the course of a CORI unit. Science observation is similar to inquiry or experiential learning, which is based on John Dewey's theory of constructivism. Learning is an active, continuous process in which students use information from their environment to make personal connections and meaning, based on their background knowledge and previous experience. Constructivism posits that students need opportunities to experience what they are learning in a direct way and time to think and make sense of what they are learning. Creating or extracting meaning from real-world experiences involves many conversations about these concepts and ideas with peers and teachers. In other words, we make meaning of these ideas and concepts by reading, writing, and talking about them with others. Teachers need to encourage discussion and dialogue about observations and interactions. In what John Dewey called "learning by doing," students make sense of the world around them by talking about it. Talking about hermit crabs is just as important as observing them. Discussions about snowflakes and how clouds form take place when student's attention is centered on these kinds of phenomena. Students' questions can lead teachers to create activities that provide students with opportunities to experience the weather or the life cycles of animals. First we experience them, and then we talk about them, until we understand.

The teacher's task is to create discussions among students in ways that enable them to work through their ideas and apply them to real-world phenomena that they then see in a new light. Teachers need to keep working with students to create ideas and must keep encouraging them to describe and explain the phenomena they observe—teachers cannot just "disappear" from these important discussions.

## Real-World Interactions about Weather

Once Margaret's class decided that they wanted to be weather watchers, she went out and purchased a weather station. She brought it to school the next day, and the students helped her assemble it right there in the middle of the classroom.

I was so excited to show the students the weather station I had purchased. The day I brought it to school I just set it on my desk and didn't say anything about it. The students kept asking me what it was, and I told them we were going to find out later. They couldn't stand the suspense! Finally I gave in, and we all sat down on the rug and I opened the kit. We looked at all the pieces packaged so neatly. We read through the booklet included in the kit. The kids immediately wanted to put it together. So we did!

As I assembled it, we discussed what purpose each instrument had. I told the kids that the weather station was designed to help us observe and understand the weather. It would also help us learn how to make the most accurate recordings. When we talk about weather we are really describing the conditions around us.

Once the weather station was assembled, we took it outside and mounted it on a table in the playground. We placed the table outside our classroom windows so that we could see it and also protect it. The students were very possessive of their weather station. They made signs and posted them all around the station: "Don't touch!!!" "Room 10's Weather Station," and "Stay Away!!! That Means YOU!!!" One day during recess some little kids were messing around with the weather station. The kids in my class were out there like lightning telling them to stay away. "We are conducting experiments," they told them.

With our weather station we measured relative humidity by having both dry and wet bulb thermometer readings. The manometer on our station measured the air pressure. We learned that when the air pressure increases the water level in the tube goes down slightly and when the pressure decreases the level went up slightly. We learned that rising or high pressure often means good weather, while falling or low pressure signals that bad weather is on the way. We were able to record our findings and tried to predict the weather.

We had a test tube and funnel in the kit to use as a rain gauge. Each day we would read off the amount of rain on the scale on the side of the tube, empty it, and start again. This was a favorite job among the students.

I think our favorite part of the weather station was the anemometer. The anemometer measured the wind speed. The wind vane was used to measure the wind direction. To measure the wind speed we released the cups and then turned over the 3-minute timer. We had to count the number of times the dial rotated past the mark in 3 minutes; then we used a wind speed chart to calculate the wind speed. We used our rain gauge to measure the snow. We just pushed it into the snow until it was full, and then brought it inside. We recorded the depth of the snow, and then once the snow melted we read off the equivalent water depth.

The weather station became a very important fixture in our CORI unit. I'll always remember one day when someone noticed the anemometer whirling around. The kids were so excited that they all ran to the window to watch. We really had a blast recording our weather data from our very own weather station. We had posters everywhere of the temperature, how many days it had snowed in a row, and what the weather was like every day in the month.

## How Do Teachers Incorporate Real-World Interactions into Their Classrooms?

Real-world interactions are centered on building sustained interest in the conceptual theme. Oftentimes a science concept such as climate, for example, is covered in about a week. In many classrooms teachers have students read about climate in a chapter of the science textbook . . . boring! Knowing the definition of climate and really understanding the concept of how animals and insects adapt in different climates can really be quite exciting. But teachers have to create situations where students can become interested. How do they do this? Who cares about weather? We have all experienced it in one way or another. How can it become really interesting? These are the kinds of questions teachers must ask about their conceptual theme. Margaret constantly thought of ways to get the students "involved" with weather firsthand in order to create new excitement about the weather.

We made graphs and charts about patterns in the weather. Brooke noticed that there were several days in January where the weather was unseasonably warm for several days in a row. She brought this up in class one day, and so the class decided to chart the temperature for the month of January and compare it to the month of February [see Figure 3.4]. Brooke was in charge of the temperature. Each morning she checked the temperature outside. She made big charts and graphed the temperature each week. Everyone loved to see how the temperature changed over time. We compared it to figures in the *Weather Almanac*. The students learned all about the Almanac. The students made charts for precipitation and snowfall. They learned about collecting data, graphing, and interpreting the data [see Figure 3.5].

**FIGURE 3.4.** Brooke makes a chart so she can graph the temperature during the month of January.

**FIGURE 3.5.** Brooke transfers data from her weather journal to the graph.

One of the first things Margaret did to get her students interested in the weather was to let them think of ways weather affects the world around them. She let students think of their own ideas and then found ways to bring literacy-related activities into their conversations and activities to validate the students' thinking. She helped them collect data, analyze the data, and experiment over and over with several aspects of the weather.

> We came up with a graphic organizer to help us map out how weather affects our lives. The students came up with great ideas of how weather conditions can affect our lives. They said weather affects people's jobs, what they wear, their gardens, their homes, their pets, their cars, vacations, traveling, and so on. Then the students and I talked about how animals were affected by the weather. We read the book *Stranger in the Woods*. It is a book with actual photographs of deer in the woods. This inspired the children to think about how birds survive in the cold weather. After their research, the students decided they needed to make bird feeders. Based on what they had read, they decided to make pinecone and peanut butter and birdseed bird feeders. We also strung fruit and hung it in the trees outside our classroom windows. The children were so excited when the birds came and started eating their goodies. They watched the birds with binoculars, kept notes on what the birds ate most, and loved learning that what their research told them actually worked!

This activity got the students thinking about how birds get food in the winter. Although some birds migrate to warmer climates, some birds stay. So, what do they eat? The students found ways to feed the birds and to observe how they adjust to the changing weather patterns in Utah. Margaret allowed the students to decide what and how they would feed the birds. She also brought in the materials for the bird feeders and sets of binoculars for the students to observe the birds when they came to eat. Margaret followed the students' lead by providing several meaningful activities and the necessary materials to stimulate her students' interest in the weather and its effects on animals, as well as to feed the birds outside.

> Each student decorated a folder in which to keep any information about the weather. They also stapled a chart inside their folder, which they used to record the temperature and weather conditions. Students kept information they had printed from the Internet, poetry they had written, notes, articles, and pictures. They knew at all times where their "weather stuff" was located. Each of the students also started a weather journal [see Figure 3.6].

Real-world interactions, whenever they are possible, are a sure way to create interest. When students are allowed to interact directly with live animals or with other real-world phenomena by using several senses (e.g., sight, touch, smell) in observing behaviors and physical features up close, their natural wonder and curiosity are piqued. The students are instantly motivated and interested; discovery is beginning, and a connection to the real world has been made. Other science obser-

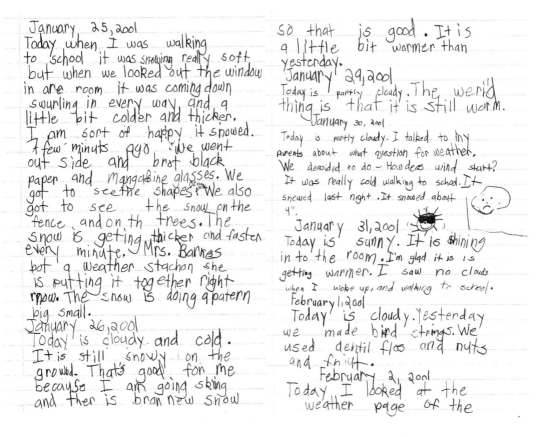

January 25, 2001
Today when I was walking
to school it was snowing really soft
but when we looked out the window
in one room it was coming down
swurling in every way and a
little bit colder and thicker.
I am sort of happy it snowed.
A few minuts ago we went
out side and brot black
paper and mangazine glasses. We
got to see the shapes! We also
got to see the snow on the
fence and on th trees. The
snow is geting thicker and faster
every minute. Mrs. Barnes
bot a weather stachon she
is putting it together right
rnow. The snow is doing a patern
big small.
January 26, 2001
Today is cloudy and cold.
It is still snowy on the
grownd. That's good for me
because I am going sking
and ther is bran new snow

so that is good. It is
a little bit warmer than
yesterday.
January 29, 2001
Today is partly cloudy. The werid
thing is that it is still warm.
January 30, 2001
Today is partly cloudy. I talked to my
parents about what question for weather.
We deasided to do – How does wind start?
It was really cold walking to school. It
snowed last night. It snowed about
4".
January 31, 2001
Today is sunny. It is shining
into the room. I'm glad it is is
getting warmer. I saw no clouds
when I woke up, and walking to school.
February 1, 2001
Today is cloudy. Yesterday
we made bird strings. We
used dentil floss and nuts
and fruit.
February 2, 2001
Today I looked at the
weather page of the

**FIGURE 3.6.** An excerpt from Mairead's weather journal.

vation may include laboratory activities, hands-on activities, demonstrations, and the use of manipulatives to construct real meaning from stated concepts and ideas. Real-world interactions are not, however, limited to science. If you are integrating social studies content in your CORI unit, for example, students can see films, reenact parts of history, have a mock trial, or divide into the Senate and the House of Representatives and go through the steps of passing a bill through Congress. The ideas are limitless when it comes to real-world interaction. Everything from field trips to guest speakers can be used to create interest in your conceptual theme. The rationale for experiential learning is to discover, to question, and to think, which is where conceptual understanding begins (Anderson, 1998; Guthrie, VanMeter, et al., 1996).

## BUILDING A CORI UNIT

CORI is an *instructional* framework. So once you have decided on a conceptual theme, which is essentially your curriculum, the next step is planning your *instruc-*

*tion*, or *how* you will *actually teach* this concept over a 12- to 18-week period. There are for *phases* to CORI instruction, not to be confused with the nine *principles*. Stay with me. The purpose of the four phases is to focus your instruction so that implementing the principles is more natural and simple. Really, the four phases give you the instructional framework that makes CORI happen; it is the *how* of teaching.

The first phase is called "Observe and Personalize." The purpose of this phase is to build curiosity and interest in your concept. This is the phase of instruction where engagement principles such as Real-World Interactions, Teacher Involvement, and Social Collaboration, among others, are implemented. This phase will be discussed in more detail in this chapter.

The second phase of CORI is called "Search and Retrieve." The purpose of this phase is to teach your students how to access the texts they will be using, including a variety of books. This is the phase where the principles of Interesting Texts and Strategy Instruction (such as searching skills, note taking, and text structure), among others, are implemented. This phase will be discussed in more detail in Chapter 4.

The third phase of CORI is called "Comprehend and Integrate." The purpose of this phase is to teach students how to understand and synthesize information they have gathered from multiple sources. It also includes teaching students how to write or present this information in a meaningful way. Principles such as Autonomy Support, Strategy Instruction (such as comprehension strategies and how to write for explanation), Social Collaboration (such as group projects), among others, are implemented. This phase will be discussed in more detail in Chapter 5.

Finally, the fourth phase is called "Communicate to Others." The purpose of this phase is to teach students how to communicate their knowledge and ideas in numerous ways to others. For example, students may do oral reports, group presentations, or a research project to answer a question. Engagement principles that can be implemented include Autonomy Support, Evaluation for Engagement, and Social Collaboration. This phase will be discussed in more detail in Chapter 7.

As you can see, several engagement principles such as Collaboration Support and Strategy Instruction span more than one phase of CORI. This is normal. Focusing your instruction on the four phases actually makes the implementation of the engagement principles easier; they happen automatically! The engagement principles do not fit into phases neatly; they are supposed to be *principles*, not a checklist.

Also, keep in mind that these four phases are *not* static. You do not do the first phase and then stop, begin the second phase and then stop, and so on. The phases are *fluid*, which means that they flow into each other all the time. See Figure 9.1 for an idea of how these four phases *generally* flow by week. You should start your CORI unit by creating interest (in clouds), which is the Observe and Personalize phase. By the second week, your students should be spending time reading—the Search and Retrieve phase. But continue the interactions and. observations (of the clouds). You keep layering the phases and then you begin again with interaction or observation of something else relevant to your concept (like the temperature). As you read about Margaret's classroom, you will notice how her students are observing weather outside, participating in a comprehension strategy lesson, and working on their research reports all in the same week. I know it sounds confusing, but keep reading and you will soon see that it all fits together rather nicely. Trust me!

These four phases guide your instruction so that your students are ultimately able to come to an in-depth understanding of the concept you have chosen. By the end of this volume, you should have an entire instructional plan written and ready to implement—that is—if you *work* while you read.

## Highlights of "Observe and Personalize"

Students become engaged in the topic through firsthand experiences in science (or the given subject)—that is, through observing. Students may then collect data, analyze the data, and conduct experiments to test their theories—thus personalizing thr information they collect.

## Example of the Theme: Weather

Specific examples of how students might "Observe and Personalize" the weather are to:

- Observe different kinds of weather.
- Discuss and observe components of weather such as snow, rain, wind.
- Build a weather station. Keep a weather log—draw, label, describe. Collect data for charts and graphs. Conduct experiments. Make predictions about the weather.
- Make a weather quilt.
- Keep a weather journal.
- Make bird feeders out of pinecones and peanut butter, and observe the birds feeding.
- Create other hands-on experiences related to the topic.

Other ideas for how students might "Observe and Personalize" in various subject content areas include:

- Dissect a frog, worm, or other small creature (for third grade and up).
- Build a human "cell" from clay.
- Reenact part of a Civil War battle.
- Divide the classroom by hair color and teach "discrimination" for a day.
- Observe an animal in the classroom (whether a bird, hermit crab, turtle, snake, rabbit, or hamster) over an extended period of time.

- Collect crickets and study them.
- Study owl pellets as an introduction to food webs.
- Observe birds and other wildlife outside.
- Examine different kinds of birds' feathers; do experiments with water and then oil on the feathers.
- Observe a plant growing in the classroom; record what happens and make a graph or a chart of the plant's growth progress.
- Watch a movie or a video about volcanoes, earthquakes, or floods.
- Plant a garden in the school yard.
- Classify rocks and minerals.
- Visit the local planetarium, zoo, aviary, museum, or art gallery.
- Do experiments or demonstrations about topics of general interest to the students.

## Instructional Design Questions: Observe and Personalize

In devising a CORI instructional plan, teachers should compose their own answers to the following questions in collaboration with other grade-level teachers and reading specialists. The dialogue attending these questions and the teachers' specific answers constitute the information underlying their written instructional plans.

1. What is the concept students are learning about (based on the core curriculum)?
2. What are some observational activities?
3. Which reading goals of the district or school are accomplished through these observations?
4. What science (or other content area) goals for the district or school are accomplished through these observations?
5. What phenomena are the students to observe?
6. How do the students perform their observations?
7. What kinds of choices must the students make as they observe?
8. How will the students be grouped for observation?
9. How do teachers support students in their observing?
10. How do the students record and represent their observations?
11. How do I teach observation and recording?

## Instructional Planning Chart for Observe and Personalize

Once you have selected your conceptual theme, you are ready to begin filling out your Instructional Planning Chart for Phase 1: Observe and Personalize (see Appendix A). The four columns to fill out are (1) Educational Goals, (2) Student Activities, (3) Teaching Strategies, and (4) Materials/Resources.

## *Educational Goals*

You should choose four to five educational goals for this phase, including goals for reading and for the content area (e.g., science). The goals will come from the state core curriculum standards, but they will differ for reading and for science. Ideally, during this phase of CORI you will want your students to learn *how to observe details*, whether about clouds, caterpillars, or volcanoes. The goals you choose for this phase are to help your students be able to observe things about your conceptual theme and to make direct, personal connections to these observations in multiple ways.

Goals for reading are more effective if they are process skills and learning-oriented in nature. Goals for science (or social studies, etc.) should be content-based. The content goals will be based on the curriculum standards as well. The content goals will be specific things you want your students to learn about your science (or social studies) concept. In other words, you want a couple of process goals or skills and a couple of content goals that will last for 16 to 18 weeks.

For example:

### *Observe and Personalize Goals*

Reading Goal 1: Students will draw and label objects for observation.
Reading Goal 2: Students will record observations on a chart or graph.
Science Goal 1: Students will observe different kinds of weather over time.
Science Goal 2: Students will compare and contrast weather patterns in all four seasons of the year.

The idea is to think of important reading skills that your students need to learn and then, in the "Student Activities" column, to think of several ways of accomplishing these goals over the 16 to 18 weeks of time allowed. If you select goals that are very specific, you will have too many. For example, these content goals are too specific: Observe clouds. Observe rain. Observe snow. Label a snowflake. Draw different clouds. Here is a good general rule of thumb: if the goal can be accomplished in one lesson or one day, it is too specific.

The reading and content goals should be broad enough that it might take weeks to fully accomplish them. Students need a lot of practice with skills to be able to implement them independently. Having a broad goal such as "observe, draw, and label" will allow students to practice this skill in a variety of activities. Soon they will come to understand how to observe details closely in everything they see. They will also be able to label the important parts of their drawings. Broad content goals enable students to learn conceptually about the topic other than focusing on discrete, limited, surface kinds of knowledge.

Also remember to keep your process goals broad enough that you can accomplish these goals in several different ways. Students may observe, reenact, role-play, take a field trip, see a movie, see photographs, and so on. They may record their observations by drawing and labeling, making graphs, charts, diagrams, posters, pictures, or by writing about the experience in journals.

The goals you select will be different for each phase of CORI. Examples of goals for other phases will be given in subsequent chapters.

## Student Activities

Once you have your goals for "Observe and Personalize," you can begin listing several activities that students can do to accomplish these goals. You will have different activities for each phase of CORI. The purpose of the activities in Observe and Personalize is to engage your students through firsthand experiences. The most important thing about student activities is that they must have a *purpose* that relates to your concept. Doing activities just for the fun of it accomplishes very little in terms of gaining knowledge. Remember, however, to plan activities that will be engaging to students. Activities should generate interest in a topic, cause students to reflect and think, give students an opportunity to question and wonder, pose a problem to be solved, and create the need to know more.

Students may do several activities over the course of a week or a month that help to accomplish a variety of goals. There is not necessarily a one-to-one correspondence between activities and goals. The list of student activities will change as the students ask questions and lead the discussions and create the timeline for the unit. Begin your unit with roughly 3 weeks of activities, or an outline of general activities, that you would like your students to do over the course of the unit. The detail of these activities will be included in weekly or daily lesson plans. Be flexible. The key factors determining whether the activities will be successful are planning and flexibility. If you have several activities planned that you can do to teach content knowledge, then you can be flexible in terms of time and student interest. Then, if all of a sudden it snows, you can switch activities to take advantage of a "teaching moment" without feeling that your entire plan has been thrown off schedule.

A weather-related example of student activities for Observe and Personalize might be:

1. Observe the weather: graph cloud patterns for a month.
   a. Make charts of the weather for a month.
   b. Predict the weather based on charts.
2. Identify the characteristics of clouds.

## Teaching Strategies

After you select some student activities, begin listing your teaching strategies. The teaching strategies are what *you* will do instructionally to help students accomplish their goals. These may include such things as demonstrating how to make graphs and charts. You might read books or poems related to the theme to generate interest. You might conduct an experiment or do a demonstration. You could teach students how to read a thermometer. You might activate students' background knowledge through questioning or brainstorming.

You might use a K-W-L chart (Ogle, 1986). This is a great teaching framework that accomplishes three things. First, you can assess and activate students' background knowledge (what do you *Know*?). Second, it allows students to generate their own questions (what do you *Want* to know?). Third, students can record what they have *Learned*. It is also a quick assessment tool for teachers so you can know if your students really understood what you wanted them to, or you now know what to build on for the next lesson or unit. An example of Margaret's use of a K-W-L is in Chapter 5.

## Materials/Resources

The last column that you need to fill in on the Instructional Planning Chart covers the materials and/or resources you may need to teach the concept or undertake the activities. Materials and resources may include books, videotapes, charts, journals, science centers, maps, field guides, books, newspapers, magnifying glasses, weather vanes, or weather stations.

There is an Instructional Planning Chart for each of the four phases of CORI. The conceptual theme stays the same for each phase. The information in the four columns will change for each phase, but the principle is the same. You will soon see how the four phases work in concert.

# CHAPTER 4

## That's Cool! Let's Read about It

During my occasional visits to elementary school classrooms (to model lessons for preservice teachers in my courses), seldom do I hear students say, "Wow, cool, let's read about it!" The usual comment I hear from students is that "reading is boring." Many times students think reading is boring because they do not have well-developed comprehension strategies, so they do not understand much of what they read. Another reason that reading seems boring to them is that they have not been sufficiently exposed to *interesting* books. This is not true in CORI classrooms. In fact, usually the opposite is true: CORI teachers have a difficult time getting students to *stop* reading when it is time to go on to other lessons.

Think of all the books that are available to read in a bookstore. Even keeping up with a particular genre, or category, of books is difficult, as so many new books are written each year. Yet, in school the selection of books is incredibly limited. For fun, I went to Margaret's school library to see how many weather books were on the shelves. This school is in a predominantly white, middle-class neighborhood. I suppose I expected to see several current informative books; I was disappointed. There were about six books on weather in all. Three books had copyright dates of 1961 to 1963. It was ridiculous. There was one "good" book. By good, I mean it had a copyright date of 1992 and had some colorful pictures of clouds and tornadoes. If this school library is any indication of what is out there, it is little wonder that students complain about reading being boring: there is nothing (of substance) to read at school. The third principle of coherent instruction speaks to this very issue.

### PRINCIPLE 3 OF COHERENT INSTRUCTION: INTERESTING TEXTS FOR INSTRUCTION

#### What Are Interesting Texts?

For students to read, they need real books—interesting, colorful, information-filled books—and lots of them. I find it amazing that the same legislators, superintendents, principals, teachers, and parents who denounce and decry their local school district's low reading scores have little or nothing to say about *what* students read. Schools spend hundreds of thousands of dollars each year on purchasing the "perfect reading program"—but to no avail. There is no silver bullet—no single perfect reading program. The truth is that students *do* need cognitive strategies to be able to locate, organize, and understand what they read; but without good books they simply will not *choose* to read.

"Interesting texts" include informational trade books that have at least several of the following characteristics:

- Such common structural features as a table of contents, index, and glossary
- Content confined to a specific topic, such as the weather
- Written by one or two authors
- Attractively illustrated with explanatory diagrams and vivid photographs
- Rrelatively short in length
- Developmentally appropriate
- Perceived as attractive and inviting to read

Researchers at the University of Nebraska defined interesting texts as ones that are easy to read, have vivid details, and contain relevant information. Schraw, Bruning, and Svoboda (1995) concluded that ease of reading and relevance predicted the level of personal interest that readers developed in a text. When information is interesting and relevant to students, they read more and therefore understand more about the topic of interest (Schiefele, 1992, 1996).

In a classroom, interesting texts may also include:

- Other expository books
- Reference books
- Field guides
- Magazines
- Electronic databases
- Literature such as novels, folk tales, and poetry

These sources of information are provided across a wide range of reading difficulty to suit various student abilities. Informational resources are available on a wide variety of conceptual themes (Guthrie & Alao, 1997).

## What Do Interesting Texts Look Like in the Classroom?

Margaret has collected books for many years. She has them on several subjects. When Margaret was introduced to CORI, she gathered all of her books and organized them by concept. During the semester she keeps the books in crates. Ideally, each group or table of students should have their own crate of books, but this is not always possible. Margaret purchased several new books for her weather unit, but she also augmented them with her own personal library of books.

> In each book crate the books varied widely by level of difficulty. Since my class had both second- and third-grade students, I wanted to have books that everyone could learn from. I had everything from simple books with lots of pictures to reference books with lots of information. Everyone could read, given the variety of books I had. That was important to me. I wanted my struggling readers as well as my advanced readers to be able to participate and find information about the weather.
>
> There were also different kinds of literature, including narrative text, expository text, and poetry, that all had something to do with the weather. There were several different reference books as well as multiple copies of some titles. Biographies were included from the biography unit we did earlier in the year. People such as Benjamin Franklin and Thomas Edison were included in the biographies.

## Effect of Interest on Conceptual Learning

Numerous studies have attested that individual or personal interest has a positive effect on learning from text (Alexander, Kulikowich, & Jetton, 1994; Asher, 1980; Baldwin, Peleg-Bruckner, & McClintock, 1985; Entin & Klare, 1985; Renninger, 1988). These studies found that there was a positive impact on learning from texts regardless of the level of difficulty, the students' age level or reading ability, or the type of learning assessment tool used (such as multiple-choice or essay questions). These studies, however, did not examine whether learning occurred on a deep or surface level.

Other studies that examined the level of processing of information found that the use of open-ended questions and free recall could explain different levels of learning (Schiefele, 1992; Schiefele & Krapp, 1996). Ulrich Schiefele (1992) found that students remembered specific sentences or phrases from the text best when faced with complex rather than simple questions about the main ideas. These results suggest that topic interest is more strongly related to deeper-level learning than to superficial learning. In other words, when students are genuinely interested in the topic, they read more about it, learning innumerable facts, ideas, and concepts. This deeper-level learning, consisting of complex ideas and questions, results in *conceptual* knowledge. When students have conceptual knowledge about a topic, they remember more. When students are not interested, they spend less time reading about the subject. Only specific, usually superficial, bits of information about the topic end up being remembered. Students who are not interested in what they read tend to copy words and sentences verbatim. According to one theory, this rote approach represents the lowest form of text processing (van Dijk and Kintsch, 1983; Kintsch, 1986, 1988).

A large number of studies suggest that enthusiasm, activation, and concentration have an important role in the learning process (Christianson, 1992; Hidi,

1990; Thayer, 1989). When readers are "lost in a book," it can be referred to as "flow." When "flow" happens, students become so engrossed in reading that they don't want to stop. Researchers have found that interest is significantly and positively related to feeling energetic, happy, and being able to concentrate. In other words, reading is fun and thrilling—so much so, in fact, that one loses track of time (Csikszentmihalyi, 1988).

> The first activity we had with the crates was simply to preview the books in each team's crate. Each team of students had a crate of books. Each crate contained the same copies of books about the weather. Once the students began previewing the books at their table, they did not want to stop. They had never seen such a variety of books about a topic and so many different kinds of books. They were in heaven! Even when I told them it was time to stop looking at the books, they did not want to stop. The students wanted to know what they were going to do with all these books. They couldn't wait to start reading them!
>
> This led very nicely into a discussion of text structure. I introduced parts of books, for example, table of contents, glossary of illustrations, picture captions, index, and so on. We practiced using our knowledge about text structure to begin locating information about weather topics.

## The Effect of Interest on Time Spent Reading

A study was done with second and third graders to examine the effects of extrinsic rewards on high and low levels of interest in reading (McLyod, 1979). Students chose a book to read from a group of six books selected by the school's reading specialist. Students chose the most interesting book to them based on the illustrations in and features of the book. Then, these children were asked to select an activity to do in a free-choice period of 10 minutes. In the experimental room there were additional books available as well as games and puzzles. The researchers were interested in four things:

1. The number of seconds of contact the child had with the book he or she had chosen during the free-choice time.
2. The number of words read during the free-choice period.
3. Whether the previously chosen book was the first book that the child focused on during the free-choice period.
4. Whether the child responded that reading the book was the most fun thing to do in the experimental room.

The study showed that students who read books that were interesting to them read for a longer period of time and read a greater number of words than the students who read books that were not interesting to them. The students who read the largest number of words and who spent the most time reading were also the ones who did not receive a reward (McLoyd, 1979). When children are interested and motivated, they read for longer periods of time and on a wider variety of topics (Wigfield & Guthrie, 1997). Competence as a reader and interest in a topic are positively associated with interesting texts (Guthrie & Alao, 1997). When students are provided with a choice of several interesting books, their time spent reading increases, and their attitudes toward reading also improve (Morrow, 1992).

I remember visiting Margaret's classroom one day while they were studying weather. As the class got ready for lunch, one student asked Margaret, "What are we doing after lunch?"

Margaret answered, "Well, we have to finish our math homework and do some more math."

"Then what?" the student asked.

"Well, we have time in the computer lab and then we have recess and then after that we get to read."

The whole class chimed "Yea!" with audible excitement!

I looked at Margaret surprisingly, and said, "Wow. I'm impressed."

She said, "We usually read in the afternoons for about 30 or 40 minutes. It's our favorite time of the day."

"What are they reading?" I asked.

"Everything and anything. Some students read novels, some read weather books, some read magazines, *Sports Illustrated for Kids*, *Zoo Books*, Harry Potter, you name it. But, everyone is reading; that time is sacred."

## How Do Teachers Incorporate Interesting Texts in Their Classroom?

Margaret incorporated books into everything she taught. She used picture books to generate interest in topics, such as with the snowflake example. She read aloud to her students, did shared reading and writing activities, and exposed her students to several categories of books, connecting them all back into the conceptual theme on weather.

> We had the most incredible experience with a narrative book called *Snow Walker*. It was about the blizzard of 1890. I had only one copy, which I read to the kids. It was a narrative story, but it was true. The students loved it. It would have been a perfect book as a classroom set. We read it a few chapters at a time. It wasn't long; it took us a few days to read.
>
> It was about a little boy in Boston and how he made snowshoes out of tennis rackets and barrel rings so that he could go get his family some milk, because they were snowed in. He ended up helping the entire neighborhood with all kinds of things. He was the only one who could get around in the snow. He even got medicine for someone, and it saved his life. The neighbors were so grateful that they paid him. He climbed out the second-story window, and his parents lowered him down on a rope so that if he started to sink they could pull him back in.

I found this book quite by accident, and the kids loved it. The boy in the story was about the same age as my students. They were fascinated by what he accomplished. They hated it when I stopped reading. It fit in so well with our discussion of how weather affects things.

About a week later Candace found an *Eyewitness Book* about blizzards in one of the book crates. While she was reading the blizzard book, she came across a section about the big blizzard of 1890; she got so excited that she brought the book and showed me the passage. I read parts of the blizzard book to the class and showed them where the blizzard of 1890 was cited. In the *Eyewitness Book* they told about that young boy in *Snow Walker* and what a hero he was. The class could not believe we had read about it in two sources! That was such an exciting thing for them to connect the two books. Later they read *Brave Irene* and made more text-to-text connections. That was fun.

One of my favorite weather books was a pop-up informational weather book. The pages were loaded with information plus incredible illustrations. The highlight of the book was the pop-up weather features. We went through that entire book together, reading and discussing every detail. The students learned that not only were the pictures interesting but the text was fascinating too.

In CORI classrooms it is important to note that the principles of engagement are woven together over time. The principles are not implemented one at a time; they are not static. Oftentimes, students will be searching for information about a topic, and this search will lead to a real-world experience. At other times, the students' search for information may be facilitated by teachers' strategy instruction, and then this leads students to share information they find with their peers. The following example is one in which Margaret turned a search for weather topics into a real-world experience. This experience built classroom unity and a sense of belonging for the students while honoring students' choices and their interest in different kinds of weather.

After having previewed the weather books, the children started talking about their favorite kinds of weather. They drew pictures of their favorite weather. I asked them if they would like to make a quilt with their illustrations. Of course they were ecstatic! I bought the fabric and we began the process. We used fabric-transferable crayons, and they went through each step. It was tricky because they had to do lettering backwards. Sarah drew the mountains [see Figure 4.1]. Brooke drew a picture of a house in the rain [see Figure 4.2]. Mairead drew a picture of a sunny tropical scene. The children had a blast thinking of how to capture their favorite weather scene on fabric. They placed their finished picture on top of the fabric and then we slipped it in between pieces of newspaper. Then they carefully ironed the paper. They were so excited when they lifted the paper up and their picture was on a piece of fabric [see Figure 4.3]!

One of the mothers from my classroom agreed to sew the squares together. She brought the quilt top back, and the children tied the quilt. The quilt was set up in the back of the classroom, and the children could tie their own square

**FIGURE 4.1.** Sarah's quilt square of the mountains.

**FIGURE 4.2.** Brooke's quilt square of the house in the rain.

**FIGURE 4.3.** The students organized their quilt squares to be sewn together.

[see Figure 4.4]. Sometimes a few children tied their squares at the same time [see Figure 4.5]. They loved it! I can't tell you how excited they were when she brought back the finished product! They were so proud. The quilt had a very special spot on our author's rocking chair for the rest of the year. The children always made sure that any visitor in our classroom saw the quilt.

## Combining Real-World Interactions with Interesting Texts

There is a strong relationship between real-world interactions and interesting texts. Once Margaret's students began paying closer attention to the weather, snowfalls and temperatures—writing about all of these things in their weather journals—they loved to find books about the questions that came up through these observations. This also works well with life science, when students have live creatures of some kind to observe. I encourage teachers to find a class pet such as a bird, a snake, a hamster, or maybe simply a tropical fish or turtle. Once students begin observing these common animals, they begin to want to read about them in a whole new way.

My PhD dissertation was a 2 × 2 factorial design study that examined the effect of combining two CORI principles; real-world interactions and interesting texts,

**FIGURE 4.4.** Chaz concentrates on tying his square of clouds to the quilt.

**FIGURE 4.5.** Three students work together to tie their squares to the class quilt.

and compared this combination of instructional principles to three other instructional conditions (Anderson, 1998). Students in the study either observed (interacted with) live animals or not; they either read interesting texts or not (*see factor design below*). Fifth-grade students were *randomly* assigned to four groups, each of which had different materials and circumstances in which to learn. *All* of the students studied and compared the life cycles of crabs and turtles for 1 week (see Appendix B for examples of assessment). There were three different treatment conditions and one control group.

The first treatment condition—the CORI group—observed (interacted with) live hermit crabs and red-eared slider turtles and read an "interesting text booklet" that I made by photocopying a few pages from each of 14 science trade books to make one packet. Included in this booklet was a table of contents, six selections relating to turtles and reptiles, six sections relating to crabs and crustaceans, one section on camels and one section on bats as distractors, an index, and a glossary. I made the booklet so the students in this group would have equal access to the same information. The booklet was made to resemble a trade book and was much like an actual textbook. There were enough booklets for each student in the group to have their own copy to use throughout the week. Their condition was optimal for learning about crabs and turtles. I called this group the "Observe + Interesting Texts" group.

The second group was the pure discovery group. They observed (interacted with) the live hermit crabs and turtles but they did not have *any* reading materials. This group was called the "Observe Only" treatment condition. The third group did not have any live animals to observe. They read the "interesting text booklet" that the CORI group read. They were called the "Interesting Texts Only" treatment condition. The last condition was the "control" group. This group of students only used their regular, everyday science textbook to find information. The control group was used as a basis of comparison to the other three treatment conditions, and proceeded in the typical way *all* of the students learned about science concepts in their regular classrooms. The goal of the 1-week intervention was for the students to find and learn as much information as possible about crabs and turtles; all groups had the same assignment but had different materials available. The hypothesis was that the CORI group would gain more conceptual knowledge and would be more motivated to learn than any of the other three groups.

Three classes of fifth-grade students in two different schools participated in the study. At each school, students' names from all three classes were put into a hat and drawn at random and put into groups, much as if dealt from a deck of cards. I had no idea before the study which student was who or was in what class. Each student was then given a number to maintain anonymity. Each group was color-coded so students only knew group names by red, green, blue, or yellow. The students knew that they had been randomly assigned to groups before the study began. I also told all of the students that each group would be learning about a science topic in a *different* way, but that *all* groups were important to the study. I asked the students *not* to discuss what they did each day with *anyone* in the other groups because it would "contaminate" the study. The word "contaminate" worked like a charm. These students took their participation in this study very seriously; they would not even tell their teachers what they did each day.

|  | *Observe* | *No Observe* |
|---|---|---|
| *Interesting Texts* | Observe + Interesting Texts (CORI) | Interesting Texts Only |
| *No Interesting Texts* | Observe Only | Control Group |

The most important result showed that the group who observed live animals and read interesting (and informative) texts (the CORI group) gained more conceptual knowledge about crabs and turtles than the other three groups. In fact, the knowledge this group gained was *exponentially* higher.

The results also showed that the students who observed live animals (both the Observe + Interesting Texts [CORI] group and the Observe Only group) were more motivated to learn than the students who did not observe. This was somewhat interesting because I thought the Observe + Interesting Texts (CORI) group would be more motivated than all three groups. In addition, the students who read the interesting texts booklet (both the Observe + Interesting Texts [CORI] group and the Interesting Texts Only group) gained more conceptual knowledge than the students who did not (the Observe Only group and the control group). So, although this was not a suprising finding, it does raise concerns about the textbooks these students used on a regular basis; this particular science textbook was not sufficient for these students to gain deep conceptual knowledge about crabs or turtles. Another result was that the students in the Observe Only group did not gain any more knowledge about crabs and turtles than the control group. I get in trouble with the science teachers who believe that pure discovery is the best way to learn about science concepts. But this study illustrated that although the Observe Only students were motivated to learn, they did not gain *deep conceptual* knowledge, any more so than the students with the lousy textbook.

The value of this study shows that not only is creating interest in a topic important, but so are the books teachers have students read. There was a powerful, dynamic relationship when students observed something concrete and real and then read more about it in interesting, informative books. I found that the students who were able to observe the animals came up with more questions that, in turn, motivated them to do more reading. The interesting texts had details and a lot of information about crabs and turtles, so inquiring readers could usually find answers to their questions. If students generated more questions while reading, often they could then observe the animals again to ascertain answers or get further guidance, at least. This reciprocal and dynamic relationship created a great environment for engagement.

When the study ended, I explained the entire study to all of the students. Some of the students in the control group were furious with me, which was understandable. But I was proud of them for keeping their activities confidential in spite of their frustration. To make amends, I let each school keep one turtle and several hermit crabs, as well as several interesting texts booklets to continue their life science unit on the animal life cycles. Instantly, all of these classroom teachers incorporated at least these two CORI engagement principles.

When Margaret combined weather activities with monitoring snowfall outside and other hands-on experiences, it made regular, ordinary weather patterns suddenly become fascinating, in large part because of the interaction between the real world and the interesting texts these students were reading—from *Snowflake Bentley* to *Wacky Weather*.

## What Kinds of Books and How Many Does CORI Require?

In a typical CORI unit, several books are used. Not only are students learning how to read expository texts, they are reading novels, poetry, and folk tales as well. In CORI classrooms students are exposed to a variety of reading materials, another way to generate interest in reading. When buying books for a CORI unit, you will need—at a minimum—the following:

- Class sets: Buy one copy of six to seven different books *for every student* in the class. These books should include three novels, two cultural books on the theme, and one to two main expository books on the conceptual theme. These books can be kept in individual zip-lock bags in a filing cabinet or in a closet so they can be used when needed during the unit. The zip-lock bags work great if you put a label with each student's name on the bag (not the book). The books stay nice and new and they are easy to track.
- Group sets: A group set equals enough copies of the same book for each *team* (not each student). If there are 30 students in your class, *six teams* of five students per team is ideal. For example, buy *six copies* of the following books: three science books on theme, three folk tale books on theme, and two to three poetry books on theme. These books go in plastic crates for each team of students to share. The number of teams will vary depending on the number of students in the class; there are usually six to eight teams in a classroom. Each team usually consists of four to six students.
- Other books used for the class library: These are books the entire class shares. Buy one copy of each of these books, which should include 8 to 10 picture books, 4 to 5 folk tale books, 15 *Highlights*, *Zoo Books*, or other magazine-type informational books, and 3 to 4 field guides. These books should be easily accessible for everyone.
- Remember to buy books on a variety of reading levels. All books should be culturally relevant to your conceptual theme.

## Where Do Teachers Get Money for Books?

Acquiring interesting texts for your classroom is a tricky art. CORI was one instructional method chosen to be featured in a segment for a five-part literacy special for the Public Broadcasting System (PBS), airing in October 2002. When I was asked for a good example of a CORI classroom to film, I phoned Margaret. She had just started her unit on weather but needed more books to supplement the stack she had been using for years. During the process of obtaining permission from the school principal, school district, and parents for the PBS project, I asked Margaret's principal for money for more books. Mere asking does not always work, but it was worth a try. I explained to the principal that Margaret had been using several of her own books and needed some additional books to supplement them. I also mentioned how poor a collection of weather books the library had. The principal agreed to allocate Margaret $500. This does not always happen, but principals can be a great ally, and even if they do not have extra money in the school budget, they may nonetheless help you obtain it through district grants or fundraising events for example.

Margaret and I had a great time sitting on the floor at Barnes & Noble looking for new weather books. Margaret spent hours on the Internet searching for interesting and original weather books; I spent hours reading weather books. Margaret bought some incredible books as well as some large new crates for these books. Each team of 5 to 6 students had a crate of books they could use for the CORI unit on weather. For the complete book list of weather books Margaret used, see Appendix C.

In Maryland CORI teachers were allocated money for books through the National Reading Research Center reading grant. There are several ways to obtain money for books through grant writing. Again, this is another reason to talk with your principal. Many states have legislative money set aside for books. If you and your colleagues are interested in implementing CORI in your grade level or entire school, your principal may be able to earmark some legislative funds for CORI. Purchasing quality books that meet the "interesting text" criteria is a wonderful investment. A large, diverse quantity of books can be purchased for $500 per CORI unit. I have seen schools spend their budget money wisely by having grade-level teams create two or three CORI units for the year and then alternate teaching schedules. For example, Teacher A teaches weather the first trimester, Teacher B teaches plants and animals, and Teacher C teaches rocks and minerals. Then they rotate CORI units and books for the following trimester. In this way, books are purchased for three CORI units (at about $500 for each unit) and shared rather than having all three teachers get books for only the weather unit. Teach your students to take care of these books. When students respect and take care of them, they will last for years. You can always add to your collection.

Other ways to procure books include book sales, discount bookstores, and partnerships with local businesses. I have a friend who is a car dealer. One Christmas he asked me if I needed anything for my classroom. I told him I was always looking for book money. He gave me a check for $300, and I bought books for the classroom. These books ended up in the school's library when I transferred to another school. Some book-order companies have sales on books, both fiction and nonfiction. Depending on where you live, some parents will contribute books or money for books to the school. Fundraising events are always good ways for schools or grade-level teams to obtain money for books. I have seen schools hold carnivals at the end of the year, put on a grade-level play for the neighborhood, parents, and friends and charge $1 admission, sell carved pumpkins, and so on. The books are *important*. CORI does not work without interesting texts. Good luck!

## BUILDING A CORI UNIT

### Highlights of "Search and Retrieve"

Students learn how to use expository books through scaffolded lessons. By "scaffolded" I mean that the teacher tells students the purpose of her lesson and how learning this concept will help them be better readers. Then she models or demonstrates how to think through the process, explains terminology, and clarifies any confusion the students have. Then the teacher gradually turns over the assignment to the students when they understand the process and can use the concept or strategy independently. Sometimes scaffolding takes a long time, depending on the age and ability of the student. Student-generated questions begin the process. Such questioning leads to goals for learning and the search for information.

The following is a list of activities teachers can do in this phase of CORI.

- Teach strategies for asking questions that will serve as goals for learning. What makes questions good? Which questions will yield the most information?
- Students should first browse through each group's set of books—that is, the books kept in crates, intended for classroom teams.
- Students should describe parts of the books and discuss strategies for searching for information.
- Teach and discuss the structure of expository books: the table of contents, glossary, illustrations, figures, diagrams, photographs, captions or side notes, index, and other features that will help students gather information to answer their questions.
- Guide students in their search for information.
- Teach several lessons on how to select a topic, find the main idea and supporting details, and takes notes.
- Teach strategies for determining the most important and irrelevant information.
- Teach strategies for outlining, concept mapping, organizing ideas from books, and taking notes in "your own words."
- Analyze the text structure of poetry and folk tales.

## Instructional Design Questions: Search and Retrieve

The following questions will help you fill out your Instructional Planning Chart (see Appendix A). As earlier noted, teachers should compose their own answers to the following questions in collaboration with other grade-level teachers and reading specialists. Their collective dialogue should serve as the information base for writing the Search and Retrieve section of your instructional plan.

1. What are the reading and science (or other content) goals that are to be accomplished?
2. What kinds of resources and documents should students be able to search?
3. How do we help students become aware of the variety of resources that might be searched?
4. How do we help students form questions and goals for their search?
5. What are the processes of search?
   - Forming questions or goals for reading
   - Understanding the organization of resources (what are the clues?)
   - Finding critical details
   - Note taking
   - Synthesizing knowledge
   - Determining what is important versus what is interesting but unimportant
6. How can we teach search processes?
7. How can students help one another in learning search processes?
8. What types of books should we supply students to enable them to learn to search?

## Instructional Planning Chart for Search and Retrieve

You have already started filling out the Instructional Planning Chart for Phase I: Observe and Personalize. Now you can begin filling out the chart for Phase 2: Search and Retrieve (see Appendix A). Note that there are Instructional Planning Charts for each phase of CORI, all basically formatted the same. The difference is that the goals change for each phase of CORI because your instruction is emphasizing different things. Different goals translate into different student activities, different teaching strategies, and also different materials or resources. Again, let us discuss how to go about filling out the four columns: (1) Educational Goals, (2) Student Activities, (3) Teaching Strategies, and (4) Materials/Resources.

### *Educational Goals*

You should choose four to five educational goals for this phase, including reading and content goals. The goals will come from the state core curriculum standards for reading or the language arts and will be different from the goals in Observe and

Personalize. The purpose of this phase of CORI is to teach students how to search for information in expository books through scaffolded instruction.

Scaffolded instruction means that the teacher first models or demonstrates the process of finding the main idea through thinking aloud what she does when she wants to find specific information in an expository book. For example. the teacher models how to find the idea about a specific topic. She says, "I am trying to find information about how animals adapt to cold climates. I know that a table of contents is a quick way to see what kinds of information are contained in this book. So I'm going to look at all of the chapter headings to see if I can find anything on cold climates or animal adaptations." Next, the teacher provides guided practice by having the students follow along and read with her about how animals adapt in cold climates. Her purpose is to have students find the main idea on the page about how animals adapt to cold climates. She has them read along with her as she reads two or three sentences aloud, emphasizing important words and asking the students to think about what these words mean and then students share their ideas with the class. Next, the teacher has the students finish reading the page with a partner, checking for understanding. Finally, the teacher has the students write down the main idea from the page and share their writing with the class. The teacher makes sure all of the students understand what a main idea is before she moves on. In the Observe and Personalize phase, students ask questions about a topic they are interested in studying. These student questions serve as reasons to search for the information.

Again, goals for reading are more effective if they are process skills and learning-oriented in nature. For example, students learn about the structure of expository versus narrative texts. Students learn how to locate important and relevant details. Students learn to take notes, make outlines, use graphic organizers and charts to organize the information found, and to organize information from multiple sources. These are important kinds of goals that focus students' time on how to "find information." The next phase will focus on how to understand this information.

Goals for science (or social studies, etc.) should be content-based. The content goals will be based on the curriculum standards as well. You may not choose as many content goals for this phase. The content goals will be specific things you want your students to learn about your science (or social studies) concept. In other words, you want several process goals or skills, and perhaps one or two content goals that will last for 16–18 weeks.

## Student Activities

Once you have your goals for Search and Retrieve, you can begin listing several activities that students can do to accomplish these goals. The purpose of the activities in Search and Retrieve is to teach students how to locate information from multiple sources. The most important thing about student activities is that they must have a purpose that relates to the concept being studied. Doing activities just for fun accomplishes little in terms of gaining knowledge. Plan activities that will gradually release the responsibility of locating information from you, the teacher, to the students. Activities should include opportunities to use a variety of books and resources for authentic tasks. Students can organize and preview expository books, read fiction books on the conceptual theme, compare and contrast fiction with expository books, do Internet searches, and make graphic organizers or charts to record important information.

The more authentic the tasks are, the more students will see the utility of them. When students find searching for information useful, it motivates them to use this skill further. Students' self-efficacy as readers and writers increases when they are taught "how" to be resourceful. These are life skills. Finding information on their own is exciting and empowering for students, and it takes the burden off the teacher.

## Teaching Strategies

After you select some student activities, begin listing your teaching strategies. The teaching strategies are what *you* will do, instructionally, to help students accomplish their goals. The teaching strategies for this phase are very important. The instruction should be very explicit and personalized so that eventually they learn how to search for information independently. This supportive process includes modeling and demonstration, guided practice, group or peer practice, and finally independent practice. Instruction might also include teaching students how to ask "thick" and "thin" questions (Harvey & Goudvis, 2000; Keene & Zimmerman, 1997). ("Thick" questions are "Why?" and "How?" questions, which involve long answers or explanations; "thin" questions are "who" and "what" kinds of questions, which have short and precise answers.) Also students might be taught how to use a Venn diagram and then write a paragraph from this diagram. Finally, you might also instruct them in the use of K–W–L charts, note cards for taking notes, and ways of organizing information from multiple sources.

## Materials and Resources

The materials and resources you may need to teach students how to search for and locate information may include trade books, reference books, newspapers, magazines, CD-roms, the Internet, maps, field guides, picture books, poetry, journals, note cards, graphic organizers, and Venn diagrams.

# CHAPTER 5

## I Want to Learn about Hurricanes!

A powerful way to motivate students to learn is to allow them to make choices about their learning. Choice of activity is common practice in several kindergarten and first-grade classrooms when teachers incorporate "activity centers" where students rotate from putting a puzzle together, to listening to a book on tape, to working with letter tiles, to drawing a picture, to writing a story. Once students learn how to rotate from one activity to another, they determine their own order of rotation. Teachers provide the activities for the students, but the students are in charge of choosing the sequence of activities, usually based on the number of students allowed at each center. Students have several choices of activities and soon learn to make decisions for themselves. Yet, as students get older, teachers tend to limit choices for students. Soon students are doing the same thing at the same time in exactly the same way.

Usually it is the high achievers in school who are allowed a variety of choices and alternatives to assignments, while the lower-achieving students are watched carefully by the teacher. Research supports the use of choice for *all* students to motivate them to learn (Brophy, 1983). When students are allowed to choose tasks, topics, books, learning goals, media, and resources (Guthrie & McCann, 1997), they can develop a sense of responsibility and ownership in their work (Morrow, 1992). The fourth principle of coherent instruction helps students learn how to set their own goals and make their own choices about how to gain knowledge about the conceptual theme.

### PRINCIPLE 4 OF COHERENT INSTRUCTION:
### AUTONOMY SUPPORT

#### What Is Autonomy Support?

Students in CORI classrooms learn to monitor their own progress and take responsibility for their choices. Teachers facilitate this process by allowing students to become experts about a topic in a classroom where the climate is collaborative and supportive, where it is okay to make mistakes and not know all the answers. When students have opportunities to "self-rule" or "self-determine," learning becomes more personally meaningful and intrinsically motivating (Deci & Ryan, 1985). When students believe teachers are interested in their progress and give them some control and choice while learning, students tend to be more actively engaged in the classroom (Skinner & Belmont, 1993).

> After making the weather quilt, reading together several different weather books, and previewing our crates of weather books, we came to the conclusion that there were certain types of weather we wanted to know more about. The students got really excited about finding information about their own personal favorite.
>
> One day, while the students were trying to set their own goals and choose a weather topic, I overheard a table of students trying to decide who would study what. There were several books on the table, and each student took turns explaining to the group why he or she wanted a particular topic. The assignment was for all to choose their favorite topic to begin writing a report. Then they would present their reports to the class in a few weeks. I listened as each student at the table defended the chosen topic. As the students negotiated the topics, Mairead took notes in her journal and recorded each person's role in the group. As she pointed to herself, she said, "I'll study clouds. What do you want to study?"
>
> "Tornadoes," answered Matt.
>
> "Okay, you study tornadoes. Bridgett wants to study lightning. Chaz wants to study hurricanes and Sam wants to study tsunamis. Good."
>
> The whole table agreed on this arrangement. I was so pleased to see them take responsibility for negotiating their topics so they would end up with an exciting report. Each person got to choose, and at the end of the conversation everyone was in agreement.

When students ask their own questions and have opportunities to research the answers, there is more "buy in" and personal investment in learning. Although this makes sense to adults, offering students opportunities to choose their own tasks, topics, and resources is rare in the classroom. Yet, think of how unmotivated adults would be if they always had to answer someone else's questions, especially from an unknown author, as in a textbook. Adults have an abundance of choices in regard to what to read, what to do for a hobby, what to do for a living. Yet, in school, teachers tend to limit students' choices in terms of assessment, assignments, projects, social groupings, topics, questions, and so on. How can teachers expect students to be deep thinkers if they do not allow them opportunities to make decisions about their learning and help them become literate, competent, independent learners?

Autonomy support is not simply allowing students to do whatever they want and just hoping they learn something. Rather, it is teachers guiding students to make meaningful choices within limits, based on the knowledge and learning goals relevant to the conceptual theme. Teachers set the boundaries for their students, but within those boundaries students have choices. These choices include topics to study, peer-group structures, the kinds of projects to do, and the timelines for projects and assignments (Guthrie & McCann, 1997).

For example, a class of third graders studied birds as their conceptual theme for the entire year. Everything they learned in science stemmed from their knowledge about birds. The classroom teacher, Ann, showed her students how to transfer their knowledge about birds to anything they were interested in learning. To capitalize on individual students' interests, and to develop autonomy, Ann allowed her students to choose any bird they wanted to study. Some students chose flying birds such as bald eagles, hawks, and blue jays. Other students chose nonflying birds such as penguins and ostriches.

Allowing students choice increases their motivation to learn because they are more invested in learning about something they are personally interested in. Although the choice is limited—one cannot choose to study alligators—there is still a wide range of choices available within the concept of birds.

Reading teachers provide choice to their students on a regular basis (Baumann, Hoffman, Moon, & Duffy-Hester, 1998). Research shows that teachers believe children need choice to develop independence, not only to be motivated in general (Nolen & Nichols, 1994) but also to be motivated to read (Sweet, Guthrie, & Ng, 1998). Teachers with a reputation for being highly motivating often give several choices to students during lessons and activities (Turner, 1995). These choices include which books to read, the choice to read with a partner or alone, the choice to read silently or aloud, and the order in which to do lesson activities (Pressley, Rankin, & Yokoi, 1996). When students have choices, they feel a greater sense of control over their own learning. Children, like adults, like to be in control of their surroundings rather than told what to do and how to do it. Teachers can foster self-direction through careful planning of purposeful activities that are relevant to the conceptual theme and learning goals.

## What Does Autonomy Support Look Like in the Classroom?

Guthrie and Cox (1998) identified four features of autonomy support in the classroom that make it a valuable principle of CORI.

### Becoming an Expert

Teachers help students become experts through studying a topic of their choice in depth, related to the conceptual theme. When students become experts on a topic, they can share this knowledge with others in the class, thus taking more of a teacher's role. In Margaret's class Max was especially interested in tornadoes.

Max was studying tornadoes. After he had learned quite a bit about them, he asked me if he could do some experiments to show us what a tornado does. He went home and made a liter bottle "tornado." He brought it to school and demonstrated it in front of the class. It became a permanent fixture in the classroom. To create a liter bottle tornado, take two empty liter bottles, fill one with water, and tape it upside down to the empty bottle at the neck with duct tape, making one hourglass-shaped bottle. Hold the bottles upright with one hand at the taped middle section, the empty bottle on the bottom and the full bottle upside down above it. Shake the whole thing, keeping your hand in the middle, then let go and watch the water spin down into the empty bottle, creating a funnel-like tornado of water.

Margaret allowed Max to share his knowledge with the class, as she did with other students on various subtopics of weather.

## The Classroom Climate

For students to feel supported, the classroom climate needs to be cooperative rather than competitive or highly evaluative (Ames, 1992). Classrooms that are supportive are places where students feel that it is okay to make mistakes, where their opinions and ideas are valued, and where there is enough knowledge to go around, not just one right answer. Self-direction and autonomy are more attainable when students' success is based on learning, cooperation, and responsibility rather than on grades or comparison to others. The climate in Margaret's classroom encouraged students to find as much information as possible because it was so "cool" to share it with the class.

When students were researching and came across someone else's question, they were so excited to share that information with their friend. Students loved showing their friends the reference materials where they found the answer to their question. Mairead was studying clouds, and everyone knew that. One day, when Max was reading his book, he picked it up and ran over to Mairead's desk and said, "Look what I found!" He had found something about clouds.

Sam had decided that he wanted to find out more about tsunamis. His weather question was "What is a tsunami?" Everyone knew that Sam was researching tsunamis, and when someone discovered something on the Internet or in a book about tsunamis the entire class went wild with enthusiasm. There wasn't a lot of information readily available on tsunamis, so when someone found something to help Sam it was exciting for all of us!

On one occasion we were in the computer lab surfing the Internet for weather topics. The kids were so excited when they came across sites that pertained to something they were studying. Sam and I were looking at a site, and we came across a picture of a tsunami that had struck in Hawaii. He was so excited! Everyone ran over to the computer. "Can we print it out?!!!" Sam wasn't the only one who was excited. Everyone was charged up. The kids didn't want to leave the computer lab when our time was up. Sharing information with each other truly made my classroom a community of learners. The next day kids brought articles from the Internet from home. Talk about engaged readers!

Several researchers have found that when teachers "honor students' voices" (Oldfather & Dahl, 1994) and allow students to share their expertise (Brown, Bransford, Ferrara, & Campione, 1993) they become masters over their own learning. This builds a "community of learners" (Brown, 1992) where knowledge and learning are the goals. This is exactly the kind of classroom Margaret created with her CORI unit on weather. Students became experts on all types of weather and could not wait to share their newfound expertise with their peers.

Margaret allows her students to struggle with problems, be confused about concepts, and ponder and think about questions, rather than just telling them the answers. Students learn to debate and discuss issues and ask "why?" in Margaret's classroom, which creates a community where everyone is learning, even Margaret. Margaret's classroom is one where mistakes are part of the learning process. She shows respect for her students by allowing them to do things their way.

There are several ways to do things "right," not just my way. My job was to provide support and help the students learn to love learning, so this meant I had to give them space; and they used it! Students used every bit of space to write about and research weather. At any given moment I would have students in the reading corner spread out on the floor looking at several books at a time. Students would be in the writing center putting information from Post-it notes into report form. Several students would be working at their desks on a group project. In another corner a small group would be designing a poster that would be used later to communicate their information to others. There would always be at least two students at the computer scanning the Internet for information. This classroom was a busy place. I could circulate in the room conferencing with students or meeting with groups to provide needed support.

## Students Self-Evaluate and Monitor Their Own Progress

Another aspect of self-direction and autonomy is that students learn to set their own goals and monitor their own progress.

I had a chart that helped the students monitor their progress on written reports. We had one for group projects too. The kids were evaluated on the following things for their reports and projects:

- Whether they met their goals
- Using at least three references

- Complete thoughts and complete sentences
- Original writing (not copied out of books)
- Illustrations
- Oral presentations

If they did all of these things, they got an "A." (They *all* got an A!)

In CORI classrooms the teacher provides checklists to help students monitor their progress with projects, data collection, reports, and assignments (see Appendix D). Students work with teachers to develop rubrics (i.e., guidelines) for what they think is an "A" project versus a "C" project. When students are a part of the evaluation process, they can also make choices about how well they perform or how high they aim. When students are a part of this evaluative process, they achieve more because they perceive themselves as having more control over the outcome.

> The students decided they wanted a way to file and keep track of the information they collected about weather. We had been using writing folders in the classroom, and they decided that having a weather folder would be a good way to keep track of their research. We chose a crate to keep their folders in, and they decorated and colored their folders to personalize them. This proved to be a helpful organizational tool.

Students keep journals, reflections, and observations on a daily or weekly basis to help them monitor their progress. Teachers may have students complete portfolio assessments at the end of the semester, which is an exciting way to see growth over time (see Chapter 8 for portfolio guidelines).

## Students Are in Charge of Organizing the Classroom

When students are in charge of and organize the structural features of the classroom, including books, materials, and supplies, they have greater sense of ownership. CORI teachers tell me their students take much better care of books and materials and keep better track of supplies when they are largely in charge of them. It's like organizing an office—it is their space, their room, and their environment. Students feel good when they know where supplies and books are and can locate them on their own.

> In one section of my room, I have a place to read that is roomy and comfortable. By the reading corner, I have a computer, an easel, a piano, and an "Author's chair" where students share their writing with the class. In this part of the room, I read aloud to the kids, we sing songs, do interactive writing, and discuss current news events or what we have been reading at home. I value reading and learning, and I try to have my classroom reflect it.

I keep all my books in accessible areas so the kids can get what they need whenever they need it. The walls were covered with posters pertaining to weather, graphs, the students' questions, computer printouts, articles from newspapers and magazines, and artwork. Our weather quilt was on our rocking chair.

We sorted the weather books into crates for each group of tables. Each crate contained several different weather topics as well as different reading levels. In each crate there were reference books as well as some narrative and expository texts. We also had multiple copies of titles so that as a group, a table could do a group report. For example, in one crate we had five copies of *Storm Chasers*. We used this book to do guided practice with strategy instruction. This book was also used to study tornadoes and provide information for a group report on different kinds of wind. All of the weather book crates were kept on the floor by each table of students.

We also had a crate of poetry books that included all kinds of poetry about weather. The students loved getting books from this crate during free reading time. They especially enjoyed sharing the poems with friends and the entire class. We really loved sharing poetry about winter. We would read at least one poem a day having to do with weather—sometimes more. When students would come across a poem in their reading, they would want to add it to our collection. One day we came across a poem called "I Hate Winter, I Love Winter." The students decided that they wanted to write their own poems. Some wrote about the things they loved about winter [see Figures 5.1 and 5.2], others wrote about the things they hated [see Figure 5.3], and some wrote about both. First, students worked on their poems in their weather journals. Then, students rewrote their poems on paper with a snowflake design to display in the room.

All of these features help students feel respected, and this helps build autonomy and independence in a classroom. CORI teachers feel a burden lifted when they have "weaned" their students away from always asking them for everything.

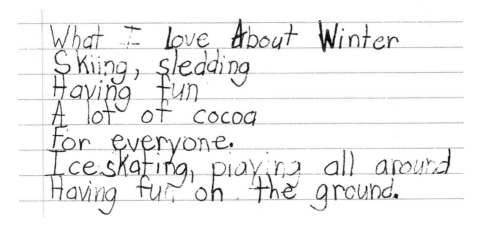

**FIGURE 5.1.** Sarah's poem about winter.

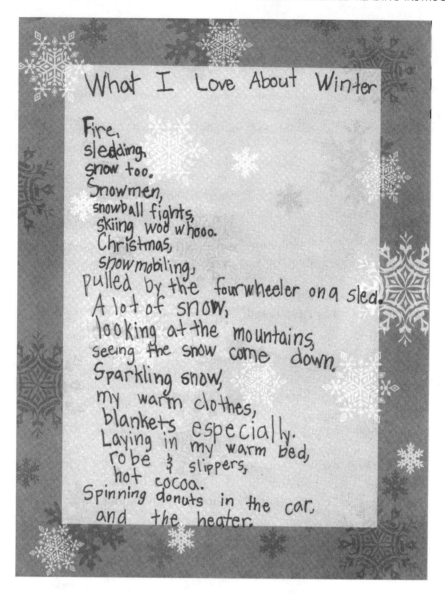

**FIGURE 5.2.** Mairead's poem about winter.

## How Do Teachers Implement Autonomy Support in the Classroom?

One of the first things that I did to help students with a sense of autonomy was to encourage them to ask questions. I began by asking questions activating their background knowledge. I asked them what they knew about the weather. I put their answers in the first column of a K–W–L chart. Then I asked, what do you *want* to know? I placed their questions in the second column.

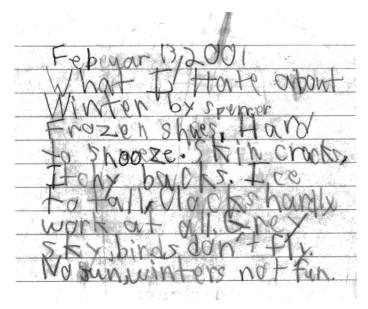

Februar 13,2001
What I Hate about
Winter by spencer
Frozen shoes. Hard
to snooze. Skin cracks,
Itchy backs. Ice
to fall. Clocks hardly
work at all. Grey
Sky, birds don't fly.
No sun, winters not fun.

**FIGURE 5.3.** Spencer's poem about winter.

| What do you *Know*? | What do you *Want* to know? | *Learned*? |
|---|---|---|
| • Weather changes.<br>• Weather can be dangerous.<br>• Weather can change quickly.<br>• Weather causes the seasons.<br>• We have to wear different kinds of clothes in different kinds of weather.<br>• Weather can cost people money if it damages things.<br>• Weather can be predicted.<br>• There are different kinds of clouds.<br>• Some places don't have seasons.<br>• Different kinds of weather are good for different kinds of sports.<br>• Weather can be fun. | • What causes tornadoes?<br>• Where can tornadoes happen?<br>• How fast does a tornado spin?<br>• What makes wind?<br>• What are the different kinds of clouds called?<br>• What causes a flood?<br>• What is a tsunami?<br>• What is the most it has ever snowed?<br>• What makes lightning?<br>• What is thunder?<br>• What causes a rainbow?<br>• What are clouds made of?<br>• What is the difference between a tornado and a hurricane?<br>• How do tornadoes start?<br>• How do hurricanes start?<br>• How cold does it have to be to snow?<br>• How do weathermen predict the weather? | [Completed at the end of the unit or as answers become available] |

They seemed to have a million questions, and soon we ran out of room on the chart paper. At this point, I wanted to capture the students' thinking; so, I gave each student a sentence strip and had them write down what they wondered about weather. It could be anything. I showed them how to write their question big and legible so everyone in the class could read it. I also had them put their name at the bottom. We had a big space in the front of the classroom, on the white board, where we taped each question. Students could see everyone's questions, and this created a place to begin the discussion of weather. As the semester went along, students could add new questions to the board as they came up.

Using the strategy of questioning completely engaged the students. They were so eager to find the answers; some of them came back to school the next day with answers. We discussed how questions and answers almost always lead to more questions. Displaying the questions gave students autonomy because it validated them as thinkers and learners. They loved being able to see what everyone else in the class was interested in learning more about. Students used the board to propel their thinking in new directions. From this questioning strategy, the students came up with individual projects they wanted to work on. I used the board to group students for different activities, based on topic. They had greater ownership of their project because it stemmed from their questions.

Researchers found that classrooms that foster autonomy have students who show an increase in motivation and reading comprehension (Grolnick & Ryan, 1987). In a social studies class, the students who asked their own questions understood the text better than the students who were asked to memorize what they read or to read without direction. As discussed in Chapter 2, asking personal questions creates a purpose or a goal for reading. When students have their own questions to answer, they read for their own reasons and comprehend more (Grolnick & Ryan, 1987; Guthrie, Cox, et al., 1998). Self-questioning provides increased autonomy and control when reading text (Grolnick & Ryan, 1987).

Autonomy support makes sense because that is how adults learn. When we want to know something that interests us, we read about it. We'll spend hours looking for the right information, going to the library or bookstore and asking people who can help us. The more we read, the more we understand, but it is because we *want* to learn—that, we have a reason for learning. Children are the same way, if given the opportunity. Autonomy support is providing opportunities in the classroom for students to *want* to learn. Teachers do this by allowing students choices, within reason, on topics that interest them, by providing motivating activities that stoke their interest, and by introducing students to wonderful books that will answer their questions. Although this makes sense, some teachers are unwilling to relinquish their control to the students. Some teachers believe it will make their classrooms "unorderly" and "chaotic." CORI classrooms *are* noisy—not because students are "out-of-control" but because they are talking, sharing, comparing, questioning, and discussing. In short, *students are learning.*

I created autonomy in my class from the beginning of the year. I modeled everything I taught them by thinking aloud as I read. I gave them several examples and nonexamples of how to follow directions, do an assignment, or use a strategy. Then I had the students practice the strategy with me several times. I had them work with a partner, and eventually they could do things independently. I spent a lot of time at the beginning of the year teaching students how to activate their background knowledge. We talked about what we already knew before doing anything. This helped them connect assignments and directions. It helped them establish a routine. By scaffolding (i.e., reinforcing by example) my instruction from the start, by the time we began the weather unit, the students were pretty self-directed in their learning. I gave them autonomy support by allowing them latitude in their learning activities and by making connections between school activities and their own interests.

A teacher's style and "comfort zone," or the way she handles her students, greatly affect the level to which she will support students' autonomy and self-direction. Ed Deci and his colleagues (1981) studied 610 elementary teachers to examine their attitudes about student autonomy versus teacher control, and the effects these attitudes had on their students. The teachers who were willing to give students control, versus trying to control the students themselves, had students who were more curious, wanted more challenging assignments and tasks, and tried to master or learn more independently. In addition, these students felt more competent and had a better sense of self-worth. In another study, students who felt pressured by grades had lower text comprehension and could not remember what they had read a week later as well as students who were told they would not be graded (Grolnick & Ryan, 1987). Grading students is a reality, but overemphasizing grades as a reward or punishment often *decreases* their motivation to learn. When students have opportunities to be in charge of their own learning to some degree, it can have a positive impact on their motivation.

Ironically, many teachers believe it hurts students' "self-esteem" to challenge them or to ask much of them in school when, in fact, students who feel that they have some control over their learning actually *prefer* to be challenged. *Self-esteem* is the internal perception of an external control, or sense of what others think, while *self-worth* is the internal perception of one's own personal ability and value that comes from within. In terms of motivation, providing autonomy support fosters and builds intrinsic motivations for learning, which in turn results in students having greater self-worth. Competence builds self-worth and self-motivation. Controlling students by making choices for them or by making them "feel good" provides only temporary comfort. It robs them of their own ability to become competent, creative thinkers. Within the CORI framework, it is possible to maintain balance between autonomy support and common goals for the whole class (Guthrie & McCann, 1997).

Giving students choices about the topics to study, the goals to accomplish, which books to read, which assignments to do first, and the different ways to express their knowledge gives them ownership of and investment in their learning process. This autonomy, or self-direction, increases their motivation to learn. Setting goals, selecting a topic, asking questions, searching for information in interesting books for the answers, and providing students opportunities to *choose* all of these is empowering for all students. Knowing the specific strategies for asking good questions, locating information, determining what is important, comprehending the texts, and expressing this knowledge is the next step in building an engaging classroom.

Guthrie and Cox (1998) suggest specific ways to support autonomy and self-direction:

- Give options for instructional activities and assignments.
- Create a classroom environment that promotes collaboration and the sharing of ideas. Teach mutual respect for each other's ideas and contributions. Show confidence in your students' abilities to make useful contributions in class.
- Encourage students to ask questions that will guide them in their search for information.
- Help students set personal goals for learning.
- Help students find informational resources that meet their personal learning goals.
- Give students at least some choice on how they will share their knowledge with others. This can be knowledge gained from books, research reports, projects, written work, and in other ways.
- Give students opportunities to share their strategies for learning about their topic and meeting personal goals.
- Let students' interests guide your instruction. If the students get excited about a topic, help them learn more about it.
- Ask students to keep a learning log, folder, or writing journal to record their questions, interests, and findings.
- Give students time to work with peers, complete assignments and projects, and share their knowledge with others.
- Provide a variety of text and electronic resources to extend students' background knowledge and help build new knowledge.
- Allow students to struggle. Emphasize asking questions, discussions with peers, and further study to find answers rather than simply telling them the answers.
- Help students construct their own knowledge through collaboration, conversation, discussion, questioning, and reading, and have them evaluate it themselves.

## BUILDING A CORI UNIT

### Highlights of "Comprehend and Integrate"

Students learn how to comprehend what they are reading from multiple sources. Different types of reading material are featured throughout the program, with class sets of books, group sets, and read-aloud books to complement the content orientation. Teachers should be sure to:

- Teach and scaffold strategies for summarizing and questioning.
- Teach students how to strengthen their vocabulary development.
- Teach students how to write a paragraph from an outline, the web, or a cluster map of data.
- Teach and scaffold how to synthesize information from multiple texts.
- Teach the story elements in a narrative text.
- Teach and practice the typical sequence in narrative texts, as well as retelling a story.
- Teach and scaffold comprehension strategies, such as activating background knowledge, making connections with the text, creating visual imagery, and making inferences.

### Instructional Design Questions: Comprehend and Integrate

The following questions will help you fill out your Instructional Planning Chart. Teachers should compose their own answers to the following questions in collaboration with other grade level teachers and reading specialists. The dialogue of questions and answers given by the teachers is the information base for writing the Comprehend and Integrate section of your instructional plan.

1. What are the reading and science (or other content) goals to be accomplished?
2. What are the most vital comprehension strategies?
   - Activating background knowledge
   - Making connections with the text by recognizing key ideas
   - Monitoring comprehension
   - Using fix-up strategies for comprehending unfamiliar words or concepts
   - Asking questions
   - Determining what information is important (including author-determined, reader-determined, and teacher- or task-determined importance)
   - Making inferences
   - Creating visual imagery when we read or making a mental movie in our mind to help us visualize the characters and events in a story
   - Synthesizing information
3. How can I model these strategies through explicit instruction?

4. How can I scaffold these strategies through explicit instruction?
5. How can students collaborate to learn these strategies?
6. What books, texts, and documents are most useful for this instruction?
7. How can I teach my students to comprehend and synthesize information from multiple sources?
8. How can students demonstrate independent use of comprehension strategies with different kinds of texts?

## Instructional Planning Chart for Comprehend and Integrate

If you are filling out your Instructional Planning Charts as you are reading this volume, you should now begin to see how these phases help you focus your instruction on different aspects of the reading process; keep going. If you are *not* filling the charts out now, you will need to fill them out, for at least the first few weeks of your unit, *before* you begin teaching it. The charts will not be as specific as a daily lesson plan, but should be planned well enough that you have the end goal in mind and you are clear on the content you need to cover in the allotted time frame. How you get to that goal will probably be different than you originally planned, but allow your students to take the CORI unit in the direction that interests them. You may find the students' questions lead you in another direction. As long as you know where you want to end up, getting there is the fun of CORI. When you are planning your CORI unit, it does not matter which phase you plan first. They can be planned in any order as long as the first few weeks are planned before you begin teaching.

Your Observe and Personalize and Search and Retrieve Instructional Planning Charts should be mostly filled out. Now you can begin filling out the Instructional Planning Chart for Phase 3: Comprehend and Integrate (see Appendix A). Again, different goals translate to different student activities, different teaching strategies, and also different materials and resources. Remember the focus of Comprehend and Integrate is to teach your students how to really understand what they read, from fiction to nonfiction to reference volumes. This phase focuses on teaching your students how to synthesize the right quantity and quality of information on their own, as well as instructing them on the use of in-depth comprehension strategies (discussed in Chapter 6). As with the first two phases, the four columns to fill out are (1) Educational Goals, (2) Student Activities, (3) Teaching Strategies, and (4) Materials/Resources.

### Educational Goals

You should choose four to five educational goals for this phase. The goals will come from the state core curriculum standards for reading, or the language arts. The goals will be different from the goals in the other two phases. The purpose of this phase of CORI is to teach students how to understand what they read. This means implementing the right strategies to properly understand fictional stories, poetry, folk tales, and the information contained in expository books. Students must be *shown* how to do this, repeatedly, over time. Teaching students to be capable of using these skills independently cannot be accomplished in only two or three 30-minute lessons. It takes four to six weeks for students to really incorporate these strategies independently. During the Search and Retrieve stage, they must learn how to search for information to answer their questions. In the Comprehend and Integrate phase, students learn how to determine what is important, find the main ideas, summarize sections of books, synthesize information on a topic from several sources, write coherent reports, and prepare to communicate the information to others. When students learn how to find information on a topic, read it, and fully understand it, the world of information has truly opened up to them. Teacher conferencing with students happens as needed. This aspect of teacher involvement is discussed in greater detail in Chapter 7.

Again, goals for reading are more comprehensible and defensible if they are process skills and learning-oriented in nature. For example, students must learn how to determine what information is *most important*, not just what is most interesting. Students must learn how to find the main idea on a page or in a chapter. They must learn how to use their notes, outlines, and graphs to write explanations and descriptions. They must learn how to visualize what they read; one might liken it to making a movie in their heads. They should learn how to monitor their comprehension by using fix-up strategies when they come to words or ideas that they do not understand. Students should be instructed on how to use highlighters and Post-it notes to help them reinforce their thinking or remember key ideas. These are important kinds of goals that focus students' time on understanding what they read. The final phase of CORI instruction will focus on how to communicate this information and knowledge to others.

The goals for science (or social studies or the like) should be content-based. The content goals will be based on the curriculum standards as well. You may not choose as many content goals for this phase. The content goals will be specific things you want your students to learn about your science (or social studies) concept. In other words, you want several process goals or skills and perhaps one or two content goals that will last for 16 to 18 weeks.

## Student Activities

Once you have your goals for Comprehend and Integrate, you can begin listing several activities that students can do to accomplish these goals. The purpose of the activities in Comprehend and Integrate is to teach students how to understand what they read from multiple sources and types of reading materials. The most important thing about student activities is that they must have a purpose that relates to the conceptual theme. Again, undertaking activities just for the sheer fun of them accomplishes very little in terms of gaining knowledge. Plan activities that will gradually release the responsibility of creating or extracting meaning from text from you, the teacher, to the students. Activities should include opportunities to use a variety of books and resources for *authentic tasks*. Students can read a book together in small groups, discuss it, and respond to it. Students can help each other identify the main ideas versus the supporting details in books they read. They can use two highlighter pens of different colors to show what is merely interesting versus what is really important in the texts and can discuss their notations in groups if the text is photocopied for students' use. Another way for students to mark text is on Post-it notes in order not to make permanent marks in books. Students can learn through practice to synthesize information from several sources. And they can learn to write explanations based on Venn diagrams, charts, graphs, and/or pictures.

The more authentic the tasks are, the more students will see the utility of them. When students learn how to be better readers through comprehension strategies, making choices, and setting individual goals, it is highly motivating for them. Students' self-efficacy as readers and writers increases when they are taught "how" to understand what they read—all day, not just during their basal reading period. In short, students are given the opportunity to learn how to do research on a topic using several kinds of books, the Internet, reference guides, and how to make sense of the information they have gathered and read. Their knowledge increases with everything they read. The more they read, the more they learn, and the more exciting it gets. Students thereby learn through this process not only how much fun "learning" can be but also how the skills they are learning and practicing can interconnect to bolster their own sense of personal competence.

## Teaching Strategies

After you select some student activities, begin listing your teaching strategies. As with Search and Retrieve, the teaching strategies for this phase are very important and will be basically the same. The instruction should be very explicit and scaffolded so that students eventually learn how to comprehend on their own. This phase, as with the others, may be modified based on your students' needs and ability levels. In some classrooms, students may need basic decoding skills as well as comprehension skills. These scaffolding process involve a great deal of modeling and demonstration, guided practice, group or peer reinforcement and practice, and finally going solo.

## Materials and Resources

The materials and resources you may need to teach students how to comprehend what they read include two colors of highlighter pens, Post-it notes, trade books, reference books, newspapers, magazines, CDs, the Internet, maps, field guides, picture books, poetry books, journals, and note cards.

# CHAPTER 6

## What's the Main Idea?

In Chapter 1 the process of reading engagement was defined as encompassing both motivations to read *and* cognitive strategies. These cognitive strategies are the ways students make sense of what they are reading and how they organize information. Cognitive strategies include the ways students process and remember their thinking. Comprehension is at the heart of Concept-Oriented Reading Instruction. There are several ways to teach students how to make sense of their reading. Several recently published books illustrate ways to implement comprehension strategy instruction very well. This chapter will not attempt to cover comprehension strategy instruction in detail, as these books do, but will discuss the several different kinds of strategic knowledge (Alexander, Kulikowich, & Jetton, 1994), including comprehension strategies, that students need to be competent, literate thinkers.

### PRINCIPLE 5 OF COHERENT INSTRUCTION: STRATEGY INSTRUCTION

#### What Do We Mean by Strategy Instruction?

The principle of strategy instruction includes several kinds of strategies for learning that are needed in CORI classrooms. They include (1) strategies for asking appropriate and answerable questions, (2) strategies for searching for and finding information, (3) strategies for comprehending and understanding what we read, and (4) strategies for organizing and holding onto ideas. Strategy instruction also includes *teaching procedures*, or what the teacher does to help students become aware of and use these strategies to be better readers and writers. Teaching strategies include the following:

1. *Modeling or demonstrating*. This includes showing students how to use the strategy, when to use it, and why.
2. *Scaffolding*. This term refers to the teacher's gradually releasing responsi-

bility to the students. Teachers provide guided practice with authentic, purposeful tasks to show the students how to use the strategy with their own
books.

3. *Partner practice*. This is a form of guided practice, but the teacher allows
   students to work with a partner or at their table with their peers to practice
   the strategy.

4. *Independent practice*. After students have practiced strategy instruction,
   within a meaningful context and with real books (as opposed to a worksheet), they need practice in implementing strategies alone. Eventually
   these strategies will become automatic skills.

Alexander and Judy (1988) define strategies as "intentional, planned, goal-di-
rected procedures that one evokes prior to, during, or after performing a task.
Strategies help to regulate, execute, or evaluate the task" (p. 376). Strategies are
tools to get to the knowledge, a means to an end. Sometimes I see teachers get so
caught up in how many questions their students ask or inferences they make that
they completely forget to connect these questions and inferences back to the
meaning or knowledge sought through reading. What is the original reason for
reading? The goal or purpose of strategy instruction in a CORI classroom is to help
students gain knowledge. When students are motivated to read, they use strategies.
This strategy use leads to conceptual understanding and knowledge (Guthrie, Van
Meter, et al., 1996).

Although there are some students who seem to understand what they read automatically, most students must be taught how to be strategy-oriented in their
thinking. Once students are able to recognize what good strategies are, how to use
them, and when to use them, they are thereafter empowered and learning becomes fun.

## Strategies for Asking Good Questions

In Chapter 3 we talked about the importance of student-generated questions.
Typically in school, teachers are more concerned with the right answer than a good
question. Students' questions are important not only for students' autonomy but
also for generating interest and gaining knowledge as well.

> As I read *Snowflake Bentley*, I modeled asking myself questions. I showed the
> children how sometimes my questions were answered on the next page, but
> some of my other questions were not answered in the entire book. I recorded
> my questions on the white board next to me. If I came across an answer, I re-
> corded it next to the question. The children were dying to ask questions as I was
> reading.
>
> Before I let them ask questions, I talked to them about the kinds of ques-
> tions people ask. I explained the difference between a "thick" and a "thin" ques-

tion. We looked back at some of the questions I had modeled and decided which questions were "thin" and which were "thick." They decided the "thick" questions didn't have the answers right in the text, and the "thin" questions were easy to answer. I gradually released the asking of questions to the students, and they came up with some great questions.

"Why didn't he go to school until he was 14?"
"How was he able to save snowflakes?"
"How did he learn to draw snowflakes?"
"Where did he get his special camera?"
"Why didn't the people see the beauty in his work?"
"What makes a snowflake?"
"How did he learn to be so patient?"
"Why did he spend so much of his own money to publish his book?"
"How did he learn how to take pictures and make the negatives?"

Believe it or not, most students need to be taught how to ask good questions. In first grade, students may still be confused about what a question is, compared to a statement, so your instruction needs to build on what your students already know. What we mean by a good question is one that yields a lot of information. Stephanie Harvey and Ann Goudvis (2000) differentiate between a thick and a thin question. They define thick questions as broad, conceptual, universal concepts that begin with Why? How come? and "I wonder." Thick questions yield a lot of information. It may take reading five books to get the entire answer to some thick questions. Thick questions take time, research, and discussion to answer. An example of a thick question is, Why do different kinds of clouds form?

Thin questions, on the other hand, are defined by Harvey and Goudvis as clarifying questions about specific words or something specific to the content. Thin questions may be "yes" or "no" questions. Thin questions yield short, discrete, or specific answers. These are the *Jeopardy* questions to which there is only one right answer. An example of a thin question is, When was Benjamin Franklin born? Cris Tovani (2000) says that there *is* such a thing as a stupid question—it is one to which you already know the answer.

We spent a lot of time talking about "thick" and "thin" questions. I modeled how to write thick and thin questions over and over. We read the book *What's the Weather Like Today?* As we were reading, we recorded questions we had on chart paper and discussed the answers that we found in the book. This ended up being a good lesson for two reasons. First, we were able to talk about thin questions in particular. Second, I was able to model how to search for and retrieve information from the book, based on students' questions.

Questions are powerful in CORI classrooms. Questions create a reason for searching for information. In Margaret's class, she had students think of questions they had about the weather. She gave students sentence strips and had them each write a question on their sentence strip with their name in the bottom corner. Margaret displayed all the students' questions on the board in the front of the classroom. Students could see what interested everyone else about the weather. Putting the students' questions on the board validated their thinking and helped students feel ownership. When someone in the class found information about something other students had a question about, he or she could share this information with the classmate. This helped to create a collaborative feeling among the children. Students, such as Sarah, kept their ongoing questions in their weather journals (see Figure 6.1).

## Strategies for Searching for and Finding Information

Conceptual learning is made easier by employing effective strategies for searching. Searching for information is a recurrent task for children in school. Teachers often expect students to search for answers to questions, seek information on subjects of interest, and look for evidence to support claims or ideas. The importance of searching for information is underscored by the fact that this skill is assessed on standardized tests and taught in basal reading programs (Armbruster & Armstrong, 1993).

There is a difference between just locating information and actually searching for it. Locating information may involve the process of gathering facts, which may or may not be correctly attended to or processed into knowledge. But searching for knowledge is the deliberate process of organizing facts or information to gain or increase conceptual knowledge and understanding (Guthrie, Weber, & Kimmerly, 1993).

The process of searching for information, in general, is complex. Successful searches may depend on several factors, including:

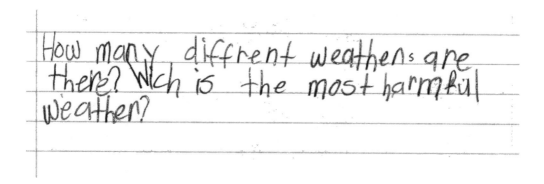

**FIGURE 6.1.** Sarah's questions about winter.

- What information students attend to.
- What information is perceived as important and relevant to the task.
- How motivated students are to read, and the kinds of motivations.
- The use of comprehension strategies.
- Students' ability to self-regulate themselves, meaning to organize, synthesize, and take control.
- Students' ability to self-question.

Searching for information *from text* is a special type of strategic reading in which students engage in the following processes:

- They have a question, purpose, or goal for reading that defines the task.
- They analyze the task, considering all the factors that will affect it.
- They choose strategies that will help them achieve their goal.
- They monitor their comprehension and learning.
- They change their strategies, if necessary, to achieve their goal (Dole et al., 1991; Wade, 1992).

Researchers who have studied strategy use have typically looked at search strategies for locating, outlining, and gathering information and how this strategy use contributes to conceptual understanding (Guthrie et al., 2000; Pintrich & DeGroot, 1990). Students with efficient or exhaustive strategies showed greater awareness of process in their reports than students with erratic strategy use (Guthrie, Britten, & Barker, 1991). The role of interest also contributes to conceptual understanding. Research on CORI shows that when students are interested, they use strategies to read the text. Even if the text is too difficult, students who are interested in the topic will struggle through, using whatever strategy works, to understand what they read (Anderson & Guthrie, 1997; Guthrie et al., 1991; Mosenthal, 1985; Stanovich & Cunningham, 1993).

Students not only must be able to search for information but, once they find it, they must be able to synthesize and integrate it as well (Mosenthal, 1987). Literacy engagement with multiple informational texts is another learning task students in CORI classrooms must learn. For students to be able to do this task well, they must first be able to search and retrieve the right amount of the correct and necessary information. In addition, students must be able to comprehend and integrate the multiple ideas found in texts. Students are more successful when they have the ability to compare and contrast the main elements of information, combine ideas, eliminate irrelevant information, and then synthesize this information into in-depth understanding. Ultimately, students must be able to express this understanding through writing, speaking, or graphic representations.

The first thing I did when I taught my class how to search for information was to get them familiar with the books. We spent a lot of time reading the books and building background knowledge about text structure. I taught the students all about text structure. I taught them how to skim through books to make sure that they had the kind of information we needed to answer the question.

I also taught how to locate specific kinds of information. We talked about what information was important and what information was not. Determining what was important depended on our question or goal. We talked about purpose and audience and other writing traits (Harvey, 1998). We practiced this over and over. My students learned how to do this part of searching well in the first half of the year.

*Three Components in the Search Model for Children.* John Guthrie and his colleagues developed a model for searching for information in 1991 and revised it in 1993. In 1997 John Guthrie and I created a search model for children, based on CORI classroom activities, with three components (Anderson & Guthrie, 1997). This search model for children is based on Guthrie's previous search models. The first component, *questioning*, is what defines the task and gives purpose to the search. As previously stated, the question serves as the goal or reason for finding information. In a CORI classroom, teachers design tasks that stimulate students' questioning through science (or social studies) observations. Questions, whether generated by the teacher, student, or textbook, can improve the understanding and the recalling of text (King, 1994). When students are asked to inspect text, to identify main ideas, and to integrate the parts together, they may process text more thoroughly (Craig & Lockhart, 1972). Students become better readers when they are aware of how different text structures change the way they read or make it easier to read (Denner & Rickards, 1987).

The second component of the search model is *text selection*. In a multitext search task, text selection consists of the following steps:

1. Preview the organizational structure of the book, for example, the table of contents, pictures and captions, graphs and diagrams, the index, and glossary.
2. Judge individual sections or chapters to see which ones are relevant to answer the question.
3. Identify, and discriminate between, the relevant and the distracting sections or chapters of the book.
4. Record which sections or chapters are relevant to the task or question.

The third component of the search model for children is *comprehension and integration*. Comprehension and integration includes finding relevant facts, reading and understanding the information, connecting new information to prior knowledge, and integrating this information with that from other texts. The more specific the search goal is, the less that information extraction and integration are necessary. In previous CORI studies students who were able to integrate information from sections of their books were the students who gained the most conceptual understanding on the topic. These students could also express their conceptual knowledge through writing and drawing. These search strategies need to be taught, since most children do not naturally know how to find the information they need (Armbruster & Armstrong, 1993).

Students in my classroom were familiar with some aspects of text structure. They knew how to use the table of contents and the glossary of a book. But I wanted to go beyond this. I wanted my students to know how to use reference books. I wanted them to read captions under pictures, sidebars, and to use indexes. My goal for my students was for them to be able to use any book to their advantage. I especially wanted the struggling readers to know how to read these books. I knew that they felt completely overwhelmed with informational books. I wanted to show all of my students, including the ones who were not inclined to read much, how to get a lot of information from these kinds of books.

I modeled how to look for a topic in the index, using a page out of one of their weather books. I showed them how to locate specific works, and if they couldn't find that exact work, I showed them how to look up a similar work or another description. It almost became a game to the students. They really got into looking in the indexes of all of our weather books to see if their topic was in the book.

Then we talked about the different kinds of print, or typefaces. This was a review of material previously covered, but it helped the struggling readers to hear it again. Kids noticed the bold print, the italicized words, and the captions under the photographs. This was what I wanted them to notice! We had a great discussion about the importance of photographs and illustrations in books like these. Some of my struggling readers offered their opinions about what kinds of information they could see in the pictures. I was thrilled that they were starting to feel confident enough to speak out in class. It wasn't long before everyone felt comfortable searching for information about their topic in their weather books. We learned to scour books for information by just using this one element of text structure!

## Strategies for Understanding What We Read

Reading comprehension research dates back to the 1940s, when it was viewed as a set of discrete skills. Since 1975, however, reading has been viewed in a whole new light, especially reading comprehension, thanks to the Cognitive Schema Theory (Anderson & Pearson, 1984; Rumelhart, 1980) of the reading process. Schema theory is a general knowledge about the world that increases comprehension when new information in a particular text can be linked to prior knowledge or experiences. For example, we all have prior knowledge of eating in a restaurant. This

background knowledge, or restaurant schema, helps students comprehend and remember a story about an event in a restaurant because of this prior knowledge.
Since then, many researchers have observed and tested ways to identify the process
expert readers go through to extract meaning from text. Research has also focused
on the best ways to teach students how to be aware of these strategies and use
them while they read (Block & Pressley, 2001). P. David Pearson and his colleagues
(Pearson, Dole, Duffy, & Rochler, 1992; Dole et al., 1991) identified seven strategies
that are consistent with successful, expert readers. These seven strategies are probably very familiar to teachers today, since reading comprehension is a major initia-
tive in schools. Several books have been published recently based on these seven
research-based strategies. We know that expert readers do the following (Pearson
et al., 1992):

- Search for connections between what they know and the new information
  they encounter when they read.
- Monitor their comprehension of text while they are reading.
- Use fix-it strategies when they realize they do not understand something.
- Learn to differentiate between important and less important information
  and ideas in the text.
- Ask questions when they read. Questions can come from themselves, the au-
  thor, or the text itself.
- Make inferences during and after reading to gain a fuller meaning of the text.
- Synthesize information well from a variety of texts and reading experiences.

Again, the reason teachers teach students how to use these comprehension
strategies is to understand what they read. How many thick questions students ask
is not the point. We cannot lose sight of the big picture. The point is that students
must be taught explicitly, with authentic tasks and activities, how and when to use
these strategies to extract meaning from a variety of books. When students know
how reading strategies will help them to create meaning, they are more likely to
rely on them when they get stuck. (See the References for resources on reading
comprehension.)

> I began teaching strategy instruction with every book I read, including narrative
> texts. When students understood how strategies worked with stories, it was easy
> for them to transfer these strategies to informational texts, and vice versa. Build-
> ing students' "strategic knowledge" is so valuable because eventually they come
> to see how the strategies are transferable. I taught students how to "summa-
> rize" using narrative text, which connected to and was a foundation on which to
> build their knowledge of finding the main idea in an informational book.
>     Early in my weather unit we read the narrative story *What's the Big Idea,
> Ben Franklin?* Before reading the story, I checked for background knowledge. We

had done biographies a month or so before, so students were familiar with researching a person and learning interesting facts. We did a K–W–L chart on Ben Franklin. The students knew about some of his inventions, but that was about all.

We started the first chapter with my reading and the kids following along. I would read a couple of paragraphs, stop, and summarize aloud what I had read. We discussed the process of summarizing and what it means. It is not telling every detail, just the main ideas. We had worked with main ideas, so this was a great follow-up to that. Summarizing is such a great strategy—and few students really knew how to do this. I recorded our summary on chart paper. We continued reading and finished the first chapter. We read back through our summary.

The kids absolutely loved this book, and I think the reason they enjoyed it so much was the fact that we were doing it together. For the next couple of chapters they partner read. At the end of the chapter they worked on their summary together. They couldn't believe all the information they were learning about Ben Franklin. We talked about the connections Ben Franklin had with weather. They loved learning about his inventions as well as his political and private life. I have never seen a group of students so motivated to read a book! They couldn't wait to read the next chapter; they hated stopping when it was time to stop. The kids would come up to me to tell me what was happening in the book.

For students to gain deep, conceptual knowledge, they must be taught strategies for making sense of what they read. So, how is conceptual knowledge taught? Extracting meaning from text is a complex process; it takes time and effort. Teaching knowledge is not a simple task for teachers. Students are not "empty containers" that teachers just "fill" with knowledge by "telling them" what things mean. Students learn by *doing*; they learn by practicing. For students to gain conceptual understanding, they must be active, involved, interested, and committed to doing the hard work that it takes to gain in-depth knowledge. For students to be successful they need support from teachers and peers.

## Strategies for Organizing and Holding onto Ideas

The fourth strategy that students need in a CORI classroom is the ability to organize and hold onto ideas. Teaching students how to gain conceptual knowledge is complex and requires several strategies. But teaching students how to organize the information they learn so they can understand it is crucial. Teachers can help students to be active in building and gaining knowledge by having them *explain* the information they find and *map* the concepts of the information they are learning.

*Self-Explanation.* One method of instruction that helps students process information is to explain what they are learning to others. In order to explain, students must reflect and think. Students can explain their knowledge in many ways:

orally, through conversations with peers, or through writing. This process is meaningful because it forces students to go beyond basic memorization of facts. Students have to understand what they have read, how it connects to their previous knowledge, and how to apply it to the task at hand. When students explain their knowledge to others, it creates social interaction and dialogue. Students listening can ask questions or clarify their understanding through rich discussion. The process of self-explanation strengthens students' conceptual understanding through the extensions and connections they make during the process. They thereby remember what they have learned for a longer period of time.

It is not uncommon for students to memorize facts for an exam. Yet, when teachers require the rote memorization of facts, often these facts are isolated from the underlying concepts that could better tie them together. Once the exam is over, the facts often vanish instantly from memory. Conversely, when students really *learn* about the systems and relationships underlying concepts, the interrelatedness of the facts and functions becomes important and meaningful. Students find ways to connect factual knowledge to concepts, and self-explanation helps to cement these principles in students' minds.

Research has shown that students who were asked to explain a text that they read showed an improvement in their overall comprehension (Chi, DeLeeuw, Chiu, & LaVancher, 1994). These students answered more complex questions, were able to make more correct inferences about what they had read, were able to make more elaborate and detailed mental models, and gained higher levels of conceptual knowledge than students who did not explain the text (Chi et al., 1994). What makes these students better at comprehending is that the process of explaining is continuous—meaning that, during explanations, students are always thinking about what they have read, so even if they make an incorrect inference or misunderstand an element in the text, these misconceptions can be self-corrected through the explanation process. There is additional support for the assertion that students who ask ongoing questions and self-explain more also comprehend more (Wong, 1985). We know that questioning is an important aspect of the reading process, so it makes sense that teachers should encourage students to ask "why" questions during reading in order to further foster exploration and explanation of the text.

*Concept Mapping.* A second instructional method that makes it easier for students to process what they are reading is the use of concept maps. Concept maps are ways students represent their knowledge, and they come in several forms. Some teachers call these maps "concept webs" or "clusters"; these help students organize their knowledge and the relationships between concepts and their functions and features. Concept maps help students understand things conceptually by enabling them to connect concepts together and better perceive the relationships among concepts. Concept maps help students do better on achievement tests because students can remember what the map looks like in their minds. When students make concept maps, it is easy for the teacher to see what students *don't* understand, and she can then correct mistakes. Students are able to make sense of ideas and gain knowledge through organizing it in a meaningful way. Students can then use the maps to write reports, to organize talks, to build models, or to represent their knowledge in other graphic and meaningful ways.

Another benefit of concept mapping is that it improves students' attitudes about learning. Everyone can make concept maps, and doing so reduces anxiety about learning. The strategies of explaining and mapping help students gain meaning from written text. These are ways to help all children learn about any content area. Students can learn how to transfer this strategic knowledge across content areas or domains. When these strategies are combined with learning goals, motivation, and social interaction, students are engaged. Combining these elements helps to make instruction more coherent and sustains motivation over time.

Organization also includes making outlines, taking notes while reading, and using tools such as highlighters and Post-it notes (Keene & Zimmerman, 1997) to record thinking and ideas. Students need to know how to compile information in a folder or a journal and then be able to use it to write a report or make a presentation.

My students loved using Post-it notes to reflect their thinking while they read. Matt especially loved to do this. It made sense to him to comment as he read. Once he was finished reading, he took the Post-it notes out of the book and transferred his notes to his notebook. One day, the students were just beginning to search for information for a weather-related assignment. Matt had two or three books on his desk. He seemed to be so engrossed in what he was reading that his head never seemed to come up for air. Every time I walked past his desk, I could see tons of Post-it notes sticking out of his books.

When the recess bell rang, he left everything on his desk. I couldn't resist peeking at his books to see what he had been writing on all of those Post-it notes. I was amazed at the kinds of comments he had written. He was studying hurricanes. He had questions on Post-it notes on every page. So, as he was reading, he was questioning. It was great!

After students had spent time finding information, I taught them how to put different kinds of information on index cards so they could eventually organize the information into a cohesive report. With bits of information on cards, students can move the cards around until they make sense and then write their report. Once the report is written in draft form, then they can edit, revise, and "publish" it. My students loved writing reports; they wanted to do a written report on several weather topics, so they got good at this skill.

The children practiced writing important details about their weather questions in their journals whenever they searched for information. This strategy was helpful when they went back over their notes to begin writing their weather reports [*see Figure 6.2*].

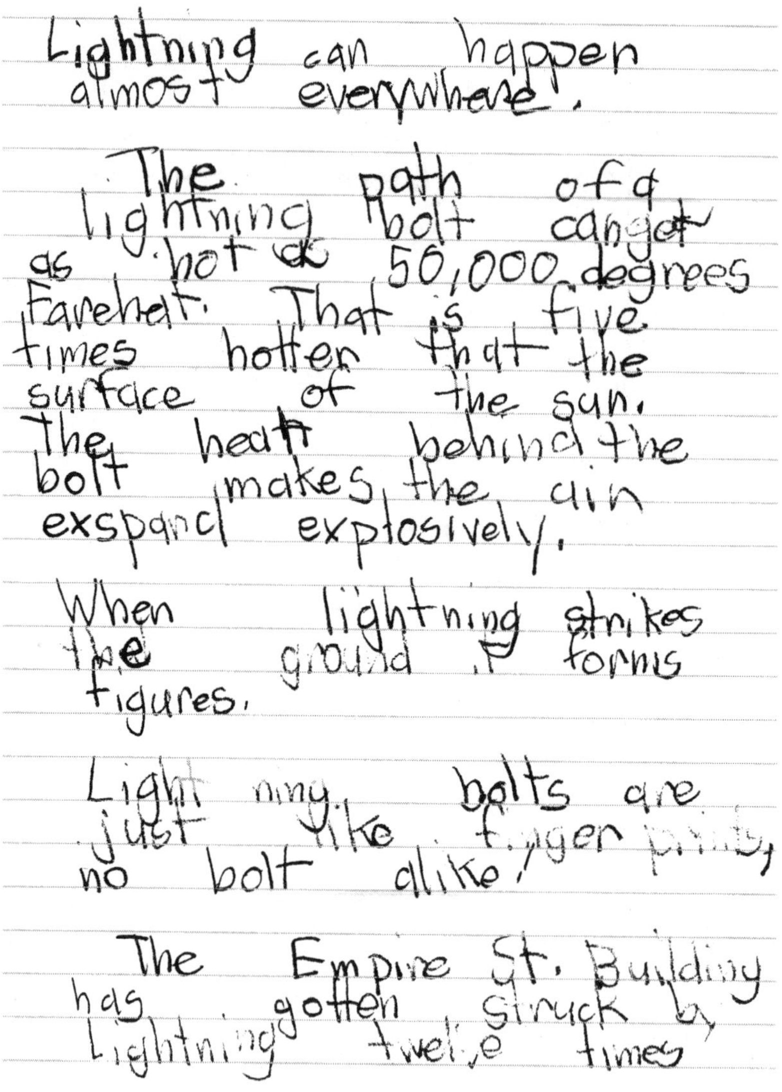

> Lightning can happen almost everywhere.
>
> The path of a lightning bolt can get as hot as 50,000 degrees Farehat. That is five times hotter that the surface of the sun. The heat behind the bolt makes the air exspand explosively.
>
> When lightning strikes the ground it forms figures.
>
> Lightning bolts are just like finger prints, no bolt alike.
>
> The Empire St. Building has gotten lightning struck by twelve times

**FIGURE 6.2.** Sarah's notes about lightning.

In addition to organizing and highlighting information from text, students need to learn how to organize their time and set goals to accomplish certain tasks daily and weekly to be able to make deadlines and complete projects on time. Part of being an autonomous and independent learner is knowing how to budget time and resources. Yet, how often is this taught in school? Many teachers assume a student is either organized or not. But, *organization skills can and must be taught early in the year* so that students develop a sense of responsibility and appreciation for time. I have watched CORI teachers year after year and in state after state learn to organize their teaching in a way that capitalizes on time. Teachers who organize their time to be able to do CORI at least three times a week also teach their students how to organize their time better. The result is efficiency and engagement. When students are taught how to be good time managers, how to set their own goals and self-regulate their own tasks, assignments, and projects, they become more engaged and more independent. CORI teachers tell me they have much more time to teach when they use this framework. It might be just the illusion of more time, because CORI takes up-front planning and organization to work. One CORI teacher commented:

> "I used to feel that I never got anything taught well because I had so much to teach. When I started doing CORI, I allowed the students to choose topics under the [conceptual] theme, and so I actually didn't have to teach as much content as before. I taught them how to do the skills with the topics they chose. All of a sudden it seemed as though we had time to go deeper with the content because everyone had a topic to study."

I try to convince teachers in all grade levels that they are really *literacy* teachers all day; they just read and write about *different* topics and subjects. When students read well, everything makes more sense; but, when they do not read well, they are handicapped in every subject. Social studies, math, science, health—even the directions to assignments or letters home to parents—are a blur when students do not read well. Strategy instruction is the key to creating competent, expert readers.

## What Does Strategy Instruction Look Like in the Classroom?

In the following vignette, Margaret taught her students to find the main idea in a book in a very deliberate way. The steps in Margaret's lesson included the scaffolding process, or a gradual release model of instruction. Notice how she scaffolded her students through her modeling of the strategy involved in finding the main idea. Notice her selection of text, how this book tied into her conceptual theme, and how her instruction was authentic and purposeful.

> Several students were studying wind and strong winds such as tornadoes and hurricanes. They were still having trouble taking notes because they wanted to write everything in the book. It was time to teach them how to find the main idea. I could tell from their writing that they thought everything was important.
>     I wanted to model finding the main idea, so I got a classroom set of a book called *Storm Chasers*. We looked at the book together and did some predicting from the title and picture on the cover. I asked the kids to listen and follow along in their own books. I read the first page and talked aloud to myself so they could "see inside my head." I read and highlighted some lines. I said, "That part is important because it tells how a tornado begins." As I read, I had the students follow along.

Now, notice how she guided students in practicing this strategy with her help.

> Next, I handed out a xeroxed copy of the first two pages of the chapter so they could use their highlighters or Post-it notes to hold onto their thinking. We talked about differentiating important information from not-so-important information or just interesting information. After I did the first page alone, I had asked students to go back and highlight what they believed was the most important part. They did this, and then several students shared what they highlighted with the class.
>
> I loved how the kids debated if something was really important or just interesting. They all agreed that finding the most interesting thing was hard, because everyone had different ideas. But finding the main idea was trying to tell someone in just a few words about the page.

Once the students practiced with Margaret's help, she had them practice with a partner at their table.

> We read on, continuing to highlight important information with a partner, and then the students shared again. Some students had different things highlighted, which led to an interesting discussion about why. Students had to explain why they highlighted certain kinds of information. Explaining why seemed to help everyone in the class examine what they had highlighted and then agree or disagree with the person sharing. Explaining also helped the kids really understand how destructive tornadoes are. They kept commenting on what was happening in the book.
>
> "Look at that house!"
> "Tornadoes form a weird funnel cloud."
> "Look how the sky gets before a tornado hits."

Finally, Margaret had her students practice this strategy independently.

> After several students explained why they highlighted certain parts of the chapter, the other students seemed to get it. I released the assignment to the students and had them finish the chapter. When everyone was done reading, I asked students to write a paragraph that described the main idea from the entire chapter, using the sentences already highlighted.
>
> I was so excited when they shared their paragraphs about the main idea. The students learned not only how to use the strategy but also why it was important and how using it helped them really understand how dangerous and scary tornadoes are.

## The Importance of Instruction in Teaching Strategies

Results from standardized tests and research suggest that elementary children have difficulty in locating information, especially with general goals and informational texts. One reason children are not skilled in locating information is because they have not been taught how to do it (Armbruster & Armstrong, 1993).

In most classrooms reading instruction is heavily influenced by basal reading programs, which tend to focus narrowly on simple texts and tasks. The "search" aspect found in basal programs tends to focus on the "text selection" aspect of search. Students are taught how to find discrete pieces of information in single-text articles, documents, or stories (Dreher & Guthrie, 1990). Students may be taught certain search subskills such as the alphabeticization of indexes, the parts of a book such as the table of contents, index, and glossary, and the basics of using such reference materials as encyclopedias, atlases, dictionaries, and maps. Often these skills are taught in isolation, and children are not given sufficient time to meaningfully use these skills. Instruction also tends to focus not on direct of explicit instruction but rather on practice and the assessment of skills through the use of worksheets (Armbruster & Gudbrandsen, 1986).

Second, children may be relatively unskilled at searching for information because they do not get adequate time to practice reading in general—especially the kind of reading needed for locating information during search tasks. Research attests that students spend comparatively little time each week reading for school *or* for pleasure (Armbruster & Armstrong, 1993). Elementary students engage in silent sustained reading only 6% of total class time (Goodlad, 1984). Other research estimates that only 7 to 8 minutes per day is spent reading in school (Anderson, Heibert, Scott, & Wilkinson, 1985). Out of the small amount of time spent reading, very little of this reading is in informational texts. Students spend most of their time reading fictional stories, poems, and plays. When students do learn about nonfiction topics, they seldom learn the content from textbooks. They rely instead on their teacher's knowledge and presentation of information through discussions, lectures, films, and hands-on activities (Armbruster & Armstrong, 1993; Goodlad, 1984). In CORI classrooms, by contrast, students are exposed to a wide variety of informational texts, as discussed in Chapter 4.

How to search for information is an important skill all students need to know. In addition, students need strategies for making sense from the multiple texts they read. While searching for information from several sources is required in order to gain in-depth, conceptual knowledge, students need to be taught how to make sense of this text reading. You will recall from Chapter 1 that conceptual knowledge is much more than factual information found at the end of the chapter in a book, or the bold words in a paragraph, or a list of vocabulary words in the teacher's edition of a science book. Conceptual knowledge includes the features and characteristics of a topic, as well as the functions of those features and how these functions and features interrelate. Conceptual knowledge is based on connections and abstractions and inferences. Students need higher-order thinking skills to develop conceptual knowledge. The strategies for searching for the right kinds of information, the right amount of information, and from reliable sources are important for gaining conceptual knowledge. Once students organize their resources and have goals for learning, making sense of all the information gathered is crucial.

## How Do Teachers Implement Strategy Instruction in Their Classrooms?

Researchers have made two recommendations to teachers on how to help children become better at searching for information in texts and in understanding what they read. The first recommendation is that explicit, systematic instruction for locating information should be provided for children, beginning in the first grade (Armbruster & Armstrong, 1993). *In many states this required skill is not taught until the fifth grade.* Think what an advantage children would have if they were taught this skill while learning how to read stories and picture books in the first grade. Instruction should include the full process of searching for information, including instruction about how to set goals and ask appropriate questions, how to choose appropriate and interesting books, and how to integrate information from several books on the same topic. Students should be taught through direct and explicit instruction with teacher modeling, scaffolding, and lots of practice with peers and then independently.

The second recommendation is to use more informational books and articles during teaching. Although there is evidence to suggest that instruction in searching for information increases children's search performance, there is a lack of information about whether instruction increases both text selection and being able to comprehend and integrate from several books, which we know are also important aspects of searching for information (Dreher & Guthrie, 1990).

Teachers build students' competence and self-efficacy through purposeful assignments and activities. Providing meaningful activities is crucial for both searching for and comprehending text. Instruction is coherent when the students see the relevance of using and the need to use specific strategies for finding information and thereby learning new things about a topic of interest. Learning is fun when it is connected to students' lives and interests. Strategies are tools for students to access knowledge; they are a means to an end. Teaching students how to learn is powerful because when they realize that the strategies lead to knowledge and that knowledge is exciting, they will communicate this knowledge to others. As the cycle of engagement continues, students' level of competence and their ability to succeed may substantially increase.

# CHAPTER 7

## Two Heads Are Better Than One

Concept-Oriented Reading Instruction classes are busy places. Students are actively learning, and with this activity come several opportunities for students to have social interaction. This social interaction is an important piece of the reading engagement model. Research shows that when literacy experiences are collaborative, peer interaction and engagement in learning are enhanced (Almasi, 1996; Slavin, 1990). The relationships in collaborative classrooms are reciprocal; both sides can learn from each other and contribute to understanding.

Teacher involvement is key in CORI classrooms. When teachers give up some of their authority about asking questions, always taking a turn in talking, and determining how appropriate the responses are and the direction of the discussion, students take on these roles. Students remain both cognitively and socially engaged in collaborative settings because they are in charge, not the teacher. Students take part in negotiating how groups work together, who contributes what, and in determining a timeline for accomplishing goals set as a team. This chapter addresses several ways social interaction takes place in CORI classrooms. Margaret has provided examples of social interaction in every chapter of this book. One of the hallmarks of CORI classrooms is that they are a community of learners where students work together and care about one another. The teacher's involvement is the key to building this community.

## PRINCIPLE 6 OF COHERENT INSTRUCTION: COLLABORATION SUPPORT

### What Is Collaboration Support?

Reading is a social process. Engaged readers like to talk about and share what they are reading with others. Social interaction can be a very motivating force, and it is a key component in the process of engaging students in reading (see Chapter 1).

Collaborative learning provides opportunities for creating classroom cultures that support students' thinking, strategy use, conceptual knowledge, and engagement with text. In collaborative groups students use higher-order strategies such as explanation and logical reasoning to create or extract meaning and arrive at an understanding of concepts. Students also make decisions, share knowledge, learn the social rules involved in taking turns, and solve problems when working with others. Students learn to communicate through language, to talk about what they need, what they want, and how to set goals to be successful. Students learn responsibility and how to make useful contributions to the group. Social collaboration is important; it is a life skill. In CORI classrooms social collaboration is another way to increase engagement in reading. Students share ideas, discuss topics, make decisions, solve problems, and collaborate for common goals.

I gave the students an assignment to write a group report using one book from their crate. There were several books in their crates with multiple copies of the same title. We had a class discussion about how to work in a group. I asked them, "What kinds of problems might come up?" The students generated all kinds of possible issues. Then I asked them, "How would *you* deal with some of these problems?" The students decided they would need to make some group rules for their own groups.

Some of the rules included:

- Only one person can talk at a time.
- Nobody can say anything mean to anybody else.
- Nobody can leave the group and go to another group.
- Everybody has to work hard.
- Everyone must stay focused on the book and report.
- Each person must listen to the others.
- Everyone should ask for help when needed.

Some of the groups actually recorded their rules in their journals.

Establishing rules for discussion is also important for student group work to be successful (O'Flahavan, 1989). Research shows that teachers play an important role in helping students develop rules for supporting one another in discussions and group work. As the class agrees upon these rules, they can be displayed in the classroom so students are reminded about appropriate behaviors when having a discussion. The following list was developed by a class in Maryland to help students in peer-led discussions (Gambrell, 1996).

*How to Have a Good Discussion*

- Listen carefully to the ideas of others.
- Contribute at least one idea to the discussion.

- Use text ideas and language in your comments.
- Use the ideas of others and add to them.
- Treat others with respect.
- Look at the person who is speaking.
- Stay on the topic.
- Only one person talks at a time—take turns.

Students need to develop these rules on their own and agree to them; it builds their commitment to keeping them. Students may start with only two or three rules. Have them continue to think of new rules based on how things are going in their group. Allow the students to make their own chart of the rules and to decide where it goes in the classroom. This builds autonomy at the same time. As conflicts and disagreements arise—and they will—students learn to develop a rule to prevent these kinds of situations. A list of about seven or eight items is normally sufficient. Once students practice their rules and get along better, they will focus on learning and discussing; following the rules will become second nature.

> Once the group rules were in place, the students decided how they were going to read their books and decide on a topic. Some of the groups took turns reading a page at a time. One group decided to read a page silently and then discuss it. Another group read softly all at the same time. I was amazed at how each group individualized their study to accommodate their particular table.

Social interaction also promotes strategy use and conceptual knowledge. When students collaborate, they check for understanding, negotiate meaning, and keep one another engaged in learning by encouraging participation and doing quality work. When students talk to one another, sharing the information they have gathered on a topic, they learn from one another.

> One of the greatest things about partners working together is that it helped my struggling readers. Since I had second and third graders in my class, they all came with different levels of background knowledge and skills, not to mention reading ability. Sometimes students wanted to work with a partner because it helped them. This was a wonderful way to have the novice–expert relationship. Then, when these students included all the members at their table for group projects, everyone felt comfortable.

We know from Vygotsky's (1978) theory that social interaction promotes intellectual growth. Language is the way we communicate our thoughts and ideas to others. In the zone of proximal development there is a gap between what one can do independently and what one can do with the help of a more skilled expert. This zone is where learning takes place. Students working together in heterogeneous groups can increase their language skills and cognitive development through meaningful and purposeful activities.

I roamed the room, stopping at each group, and listened. It was so exciting. They were so enthusiastic about their books. The group reading *Pink Snow and Other Weird Weather* couldn't put the book down and couldn't wait to share the information in the book. As soon as I approached their table, they all started telling me about what they had read. One student asked me, "How can we share this information with everyone else?" I encouraged them to be creative with their projects. Shown on the facing page are the notes from Mairead's weather journal about what her group discovered about weird weather [*see Figure 7.1*].

The reason social collaboration is beneficial is that when a group of students gets together to discuss a topic, such as hurricanes, not everyone in the group will possess the same background knowledge. Some students will disagree with or be confused by what other students say about hurricanes. This disagreement or confusion is what Vygotsky called cognitive conflict, and this is exactly what students need to force them to think and debate an issue until understanding is achieved. Through these social interactions, meaning is mediated, thinking is extended, and conceptual learning takes place.

Each group was unique in the way its members decided to communicate their knowledge and information with others. One group made a big poster. They divided up the work. It was so rewarding to watch this group of second and third graders get so excited to share their information. The members of each table worked together for the entire weather unit. They liked working with one another. It wasn't always perfect, but they learned how to work out their differences. Over the course of the unit, they created pictures, wrote reports and illustrated them, answered questions from their fellow students, made models, shared experiments, kept journals, and wrote books. Shown below is one group of students sharing their knowledge about hurricanes with the class. Each made a picture and explained one aspect of hurricanes. Everyone got a turn to explain what he or she learned [*see Figure 7.2*].

## What Does Collaboration Support Look Like in the Classroom?

Social collaboration may take several forms in a CORI classroom. The form this collaboration takes depends on the teacher and the students, but CORI classrooms cannot work without social interaction. Students talk to one another, share ideas, solve problems, make decisions, and work together to meet common goals. Social interaction begins with the goals the teacher sets in planning a unit of instruction, namely, the Student Activities column of the Instructional Planning Chart for each phase of CORI. The purpose behind each activity originates with the goals for reading, writing, and the content area. The activities are successful when they build competence and when students feel supported.

One of my goals was to teach the kids how to find a lot of information from several resources. I wanted them to go beyond the encyclopedia, so I started by

A tornado is hot and cold
air put together
Did you know it can snow
pink snow? Well, it can
because when wind picks
up dark pink gust it carys
it to snow clouds and then
it snows pink snow.
One time it even snowed frogs.
in france in 1933. Poeple would
wonder how it rained water
animals? It was cossed
by a water spout" said syintiot.
In 1974 a tornado nocked
down a farm house, but there
was a box of un cracked
eggs a miron and Christmas
ordinints. Syintists are wondering
how this bappend. In kansis
a torndo hit three times in
three years the wiend
thang is it happend May 20
every year. Roy sullivan
was struck by lightning 7
times and never died. The
biggest snow fake

was 15" long that is as big
as a dinner plate.
One time they saw a hailstone
so big a turtle was frozen in
it.
So next time it rains
were a helmet who knows
a toed might fall on you.

**FIGURE 7.1.** Mairead's notes for her group report on *Pink Snow and Other Weird Weather*.

**FIGURE 7.2.** A group of students sharing their knowledge about hurricanes in a class poster presentation.

having them work in groups and do a group report. I taught them how to write a report by teaching each phase of writing one at a time. First I taught them how to read the books for information and how to capture and retain their thinking on Post-it notes. Then I taught them to take notes in their own words from their Post-it notes and from the book. Next I taught them to transfer these ideas onto index cards. This took months, but for the most part eventually everyone could do this independently.

As they showed interest in working with a partner or with their group, I taught them how to put their ideas together with someone else's to make a report. This became fun for them because they learned that two heads were better than one. They figured out how to divide the work so they didn't duplicate their efforts. They figured out how to talk about each subtopic and agree before moving on. They negotiated what things meant, and if they didn't know they asked another peer. They learned to depend on one another.

The degree of social interaction or collaboration depends, of course, on the activity. Some activities, such as the snowflake watch, are done as an entire class. This is a case where students are discovering; interacting and talking are a huge part of that process. Other whole-class activities include shared readings, teacher modeling of experiments or demonstrations, strategy lessons, and role playing in front of the class.

Through the scaffolding process, students gradually learn to work independently; yet, paradoxically, students learn *more* when they are working with a partner

or in a group. One example of this is an idea circle. Idea circles are similar to literature circles, the chief difference being that students discuss concepts rather than
character development and themes in idea circles. Guthrie and McCann (1997) defined idea circles as peer-led small-group discussions of concepts based on the
reading of multiple text sources. Idea circles help students understand, challenge,
and question information about a concept in the text. Literature circles focus on
one story or chapter of a book, while idea circles focus on integrating information
about a concept, such as tornadoes, from multiple books and sources. The purpose of idea circles is to increase conceptual knowledge through discussion and
debate. Idea circles work best with three to six students.

When Margaret assigned group reports on one topic, idea circles were the result. First, students had to decide on the topic through careful negotiation among
members of the group. Then, as they read and gathered information about the
topic, they discussed it together. When a member of the group was confused or did
not understand what something meant, the group talked about it and students
shared their ideas about what they thought until a consensus was reached. By way
of contrast, in literature circles, others' points of view about characters and themes
are *encouraged* (Guthrie & McCann, 1996). Another way of incorporating purposeful group work is through literature circles and reciprocal teaching—students taking turns "teaching" the group (e.g., students in a small group discussing characters and events in a story).

## How Do Teachers Implement Collaboration Support in Their Classroom?

A community of learners is built and developed from the first day of school on-
wards. Margaret started at the very beginning of the year to teach students how to
work together. She became seasoned at doing this.

> From the first day of school, I began to build a community of learners. I knew if
> I could do this, teaching would be easier and the students would learn more. I
> told my students that I only had one rule in my classroom: to respect the rights
> of others. I told them that together we could think of things that we could add
> to our list of classroom rules, but I needed them to understand what respecting
> the rights of others meant. I asked them what "respect" meant to them. We
> had a long discussion about this for several days. I read books and gave exam-
> ples of how people show respect toward others. We role-played lots of situations
> so the students could see how it felt to be left out, made fun of, teased, and
> hurt. They did not like it! We talked about what to do if they did not under-
> stand something or didn't know how to do something. I told them that I
> thought asking for help was a sign of intelligence. I told them that it is okay to
> make mistakes because that's how we learn.
>
> We talked about the importance of being different and how neat it is to be
> different. I explained to them that we are all good at something, but we don't
> all have to be good at everything! I gave as an example how I like to sew. I am

a good seamstress and have made several dresses and clothes—but my sister has a hard time even threading a needle! On the other hand, my sister is good at lots of things. She knows everything about art history. She loves to draw and paint. She is a wonderful artist. I talked about how much my sister and I like each other because we can teach each other how to do different things. We also have things in common, and that is why we have so much fun together.

I told the students that our class is like a family. We would be spending the entire year together, and so we needed to learn how to get along. We talked about families and siblings and how they solve problems in their families. We talked about how lucky they are to have families and a mom and/or a dad and siblings. They care about us. Our class is a place where we spend a lot of time. It's our job to work together. We talked about the Golden Rule. Keeping the Golden Rule would help us like each other, just as we like our families. I remember telling my class: "We all like each other in here. We are all friends. We all care about each other and will learn how to respect each other so we can do good work. We have the best class. We are smart and creative and can all add something special to this class. Let's remember this."

I spent about 10 days really convincing the kids that they were in the best place because of each other. This language has worked for me every year. Although I don't ever have "perfect" classes, we learn to get along because I set it up that way. I learned from my own experience that teaching was so much harder when my students did not learn how to get along. Ugh! Those were the hard years!

## PRINCIPLE 7 OF COHERENT INSTRUCTION: TEACHER INVOLVEMENT

I think it all comes down to teacher attitude. If you tell the class they are the best class you have ever had, they *will* be. Students rise to the occasion.

Teacher involvement varies to some degree in CORI classrooms. Some teachers have a difficult time giving up their control. This takes time. Not every teacher has the same comfort level in doing so. This is okay. When you teach with CORI principles, that will change, because when students are given autonomy and support to be self-directed, great things happen. Teacher involvement increases student engagement (Slanner, Wellborn, & Connell, 1990). Teachers can be involved in several ways. You have seen Margaret's involvement with her students in every phase of CORI and with every principle. The following are some ways to support your students as they learn.

- Provide the children an opportunity to follow their own area of interest within a broad topic.
- Provide a variety of learning materials and sources.

- Teach and encourage students to interact with one another.
- Teach questioning. Questions make students investigators. Questions enable *all* students to learn.
- Provide students choice. Let them choose topics within a wide range of possibilities. Let them choose the way they communicate their knowledge to others. Let them make their own group rules. Let them make their own charts. Let them choose the book for book club or literature circles.
- Allow students as much time as they need to work on a project as long as they continue to make progress and reach their goals.
- Research together in the computer lab. Help the students find interesting web sites, or actually join them in their search (this is how Margaret and Steven found tsunamis).
- Conference with your students individually and as small-team groups to discuss progress and problems.
- Model strategies. Think aloud. Bring your own reading in and model your thinking, using what you are reading at home; it teaches your students that you really value reading.
- Let students have the option of working on their projects whenever they have free time at lunch, recess, and when other work is completed.
- Read with students in their books.
- Conference with students to set goals and check progress.
- If they can't find something, help your students, search together, or tell them you will try to find what they are looking for (search the Internet, check at the bookstore, look through reference books). The majority of the time do this *with* the students.

## How Much Time Does a Teacher Spend Doing CORI?

We spent at least an hour to an hour and a half on CORI everyday. Kids spent any free time they had working on projects when we got that far. There were other times during the day when what we were doing tied into CORI. For example, computer lab, writing time, reading, calendar and morning business, read-alouds—it all kind of overlapped.

The time spent in doing CORI depends on your own schedule and the school schedule. Many CORI teachers use their language arts block to do CORI. Other teachers use their science or social studies time. Some teachers use a combination of both. The key is being flexible.

I spent a *ton* of time up front preparing for my units on butterflies (life cycles) and weather. CORI takes a lot of time to think through the phases and think of meaningful activities and finding all of the books. But the framework made a difference in my teaching. I had a plan. I had goals. It was actually easier for me to stay focused. I followed my plans for my CORI unit pretty closely. But if it snowed or if the students got excited about a book we read, this led us in another direction. The fun part was when the students got excited about something I did not expect. So, I let their excitement drive my instruction. This made it so much more fun for me. I was learning too.

## BUILDING A CORI UNIT

### Highlights of "Communicate to Others"

Students engage in various activities to share what they have learned. Sharing knowledge happens throughout the CORI unit, not just at the end. Students share information they gather while observing, while they search and find information, and while they are making sense of what they read. Communicating to others creates a classroom climate that is motivating because the atmosphere is collaborative rather than competitive. There is enough knowledge for everyone, and sharing it benefits the whole class. Students communicate to others in a variety of ways. This is the phase of CORI that allows students to express their knowledge in ways that are unique to their personality and strengths. Some ways for students to communicate include:

- Writing reports.
- Making informational posters.
- Publishing results from experiments, surveys, and so on.
- Creating dioramas illustrating a biome theme (whether rain forest, grassland, or desert) with researched notes.
- Inventing an animal to suit the particular biome studied, and describing and illustrating it in a poster.
- Making a class quilt from drawings of a favorite animal or concept chosen for study.
- Making a class book on the topic.
- Writing about a story or book.
- Sharing team or class projects with another grade or with parents.
- Making a video presentation.
- Using paper maché to make an artistic display of knowledge about a concept or concepts.

### Instructional Design Questions: Communicate to Others

The following questions will help you fill out your Instructional Planning Chart. Teachers compose their own answers to the following questions in collaboration with other grade-level teachers and reading specialists. The dialogue surrounding the questions and the specific answers given by the teachers help form the informational base for writing the Communicate to Others section of your instructional plan.

1. What are the reading/science (or other content) goals to be accomplished?
2. What are topics and concepts students can explain during the unit?

## Instructional Planning Chart for Communicate to Others

Now you see how these phases help focus your instruction on different aspects of the reading process. Your other three phases of Instructional Planning Charts should be mostly filled out. Now you can begin filling out the Instructional Planning Chart for Phase 4: Communicate to Others (see Appendix A). Again, different goals translate to different student activities, different teaching strategies, and also different materials and resources. Keep in mind that the focus of Communicate to Others is to teach your students how to express their knowledge to others. This phase focuses on teaching your students how to speak, write, draw, graph, do reports and projects, and express their knowledge through creative ways to others. Let the students think of ways they want to do this. You will be surprised at what they come up with. I once had an advanced-placement high school history teacher who gave her students the choice of how to teach the first 14 Amendments to the U.S. Constitution to the class. She was shocked at how they rose to the occasion. One student devised a computer game and made 15 copies of it. The whole class went to the computer lab and took turns playing the game. It was fabulous. Oftentimes, when given a choice, students will surpass teachers' greatest expectations. This is the result of *reading engagement*.

The four columns to fill out are (1) Educational Goals, (2) Student Activities, (3) Teaching Strategies, and (4) Materials/Resources.

### Educational Goals

You should choose four to five educational goals for this phase. The goals will come from the state core curriculum standards for reading and the language arts. These goals may be writing-intensive, as students often do research reports, write poetry, or write explanations about what they have learned about the theme. Students may also draw and label in Observe and Personalize, which is a great way to communicate to others. This phase may also involve the art or drama teacher. Many culminating projects at the end of the semester are fun when they involve making things out of clay, paper maché, paint, and the like. Sometimes a class play or reenactment is a culminating project put on for parents and younger grades. Have fun!

Goals for science (or social studies) should be content-based. The content goals will be based on the curriculum standards as well. The content goals will be specific things you want your students to express knowledge about in your science (or social studies) concept. Remember, your students will be communicating to others for 16 to 18 weeks but in numerous ways. Many times their communication will be discussion, while some projects will be extraordinarily complex, taking weeks to finish, and others will be relatively simple, requiring much less time.

## Student Activities

Once you have your goals set for Communicate to Others, you can begin listing several activities that students can undertake to accomplish these goals.

## Teaching Strategies

After you select the activities for students to write, speak, and express their knowledge and ideas, you should settle on the appropriate teaching strategies for helping them communicate. This might include instruction about how to work in a literature circle, contributing relevant ideas and listening to others' ideas. Writer's workshop is another instructional process that teachers may teach during this phase. Students learn the process of drafting, revising, peer or teacher conferencing, editing, and finally publishing. These steps prepare students of all grade levels to succeed in school and in their future lives in the workplace.

## Materials and Resources

The materials and resources you may need may include anything that will help your students express their ideas. Such materials might include posterboard, art supplies, videotapes, audio equipment, and so on.

# CHAPTER 8

## Beyond Gold Stars and Candy Bars

This chapter will examine several methods of evaluating student progress that both promote and maintain engagement. At a time when high-stakes testing makes teachers feel pressured to increase students' reading scores, the issues surrounding evaluation are especially important. Which form of evaluation is best? How can you tell? What if that form of assessment does not work for my English as a Second Language (ESL) student? How do I assess my students fairly? Why is so much emphasis placed on end-of-level tests? How do I handle pressure from parents? This chapter will address these issues and concerns. The issue of evaluation is an important one for all teachers, parents, and students.

Closely tied to evaluation is the question of rewarding and praising students. Striking a balance between rewards and praise in relation to other forms of assessment is crucial in maintaining engagement. The issue of rewards and praise is one that can be misunderstood. Rewards and praise can either help or hinder student engagement. Remember the vignette about Margaret's classroom waiting to get into the ice skating performance when it suddenly began to snow? How did she get kids from Utah, where it snows all winter long, to get excited about snowflakes? This chapter will address how to raise standardized test scores, but it does not happen with gold stars or candy bars; in fact, that may be the very thing that drives kids from learning.

### PRINCIPLE 8 OF COHERENT INSTRUCTION: EVALUATION FOR ENGAGEMENT

### What Is Evaluation for Engagement?

Evaluation is part of every classroom at every grade level. There is no way to get around grades. But the way teachers evaluate students can either foster or hinder reading engagement. If teachers are to be effective, they need to be strategic in their methods of assessment. An engaged teacher is committed to her students' success. This level of commitment requires both reflection and special effort to meet the diverse needs of all her students (Leipzig & Afflerbach, 2000). Teaching is hard work—there is no doubt of that. But engaged teachers thrive on the challenge of meeting students' needs. In CORI classrooms evaluation may take any of several forms.

## Effort versus Absolute Standards

Evaluation is meant to emphasize student progress and achievement rather than to establish an absolute standard (Guthrie et al., 2000). In Chapter 7 competition was discussed in terms of social support and collaboration. Even in collaborative settings, when students are compared to one another, there is competition. In all competitions there is a winner and a loser. In this case, when grading is done on an absolute standard, only the high achievers win, while all the other students lose. Since no one likes to lose, this method of evaluation motivates only the high achievers in a positive way. On the other hand, when teachers evaluate *the entire class* on its progress, everyone can win. Everyone can be successful and improve. Also, by doing this, effort is rewarded, not just ability. The key to improvement is in setting goals. Both teachers and students can set goals for learning and improving, as discussed in Chapter 2.

## Goals Determine Evaluation

The methods of evaluation should be closely aligned with the goals of the instruction and the curriculum or content that students are required to learn. Goals determine which kinds of assessment we use and how often we assess our students. I teach goal setting and evaluation at the beginning of the semester and spend 16 weeks illustrating that the goals we choose for learning must strongly take into account the "kinds" of assessment and evaluation we intend to use to achieve and maintain reading engagement. As the semester progresses, teachers' traditional views of assessment are challenged and perhaps reanalyzed until they find ways to evaluate their own teaching in ways that are meaningful not only to themselves as teachers but also to the students' long-term progress and improvement. Teachers become more reflective and find more meaningful ways to build new knowledge from what their students currently understand.

Leipzig and Afflerbach (2000) offer the CURRV (Consequences, Usefulness, Roles, Reliability, and Validity) framework that teachers or administrators can use to evaluate the kinds of reading assessments given to students. The framework helps teachers consider the following:

1. What are the *consequences* of the assessment?
2. What is the *usefulness* of the assessment?
3. What are the roles of both the teacher and the student in the assessment?

4. What is the *reliability* of the assessment?
5. What is the *validity* of the assessment?

Although there are many ways to assess students' abilities, there is a lot of information available to help teachers, administrators, or curriculum specialists make informed decisions.

## Continuous Evaluation Informs Instruction

One of the most important aspects of our job, as teachers, is the relationship between assessment, curriculum, and instruction. If we are not constantly evaluating our teaching in relation to what our students are *achieving*, we may be wasting precious time. Yet, when we fully appreciate what our students *know* and *can do*, we can build usefully upon this knowledge in great ways. As students show progress, we can celebrate the success they have. This progress can then guide the curriculum we use and the methods of instruction we employ. Ideally, evaluation should inform our teaching methods and motivate our students to learn. All too often, evaluation is seen as a burden—a time-consuming task that *must* be done at the beginning and end of the year. If teachers view evaluation as just one key culminating test, they will probably not use assessment sufficiently throughout the year to inform their instructional habits. At the same time, their instruction will probably not be meeting the needs of all the students. And, as important consequences, the students will not enjoy learning and the teacher will not enjoy teaching.

## Evaluate the Child's Strengths

Evaluation informs instruction best when it gives us a complete picture of what our students can do in all areas. If we are left to rely solely on last year's end-of-level test scores, we are at a loss for guidance. For evaluation to be successful it needs to be done in multiple ways in multiple settings to properly get at students' strengths. After all, aren't we as interested in what our students *know and can do* as we are in the obverse? Often teachers operate on the basis of a deficit model of assessment. Teachers test students and learn what they missed or what they cannot do, and then the teachers try to teach them what was missed. Working from a deficit model is a poor way to go about building knowledge. Instruction is much more successful when teachers are able to build on students' knowledge and then *extend it*. Therefore, students are best evaluated in the following ways:

• *Strategy or skill assessment*. Teachers model, scaffold, and provide practice in seeking out information, and then eventually students are able to use such strategies independently to help themselves find information, understand what they read, or help themselves in other ways. Knowing *what* strategy to use and *when* can be assessed often.

• *Authentic tasks*. Teachers who give students authentic assignments can assess whether or not their students are applying strategic knowledge to these tasks. The goal is for students to use the knowledge and skills they learn in their everyday lives. Assessment is made easier for both teachers and students when it reflects an authentic context for using the skill.

• *Students' writing.* Writing can be evaluated by having students keep logs or journals to record their ideas and thinking. Students' daily writing tells us so much about what they know and can do on several levels, from spelling to idea formation to conceptual understanding.

• *Oral reports.* We know what students understand through their ability to explain their knowledge to others. Oral reports are a great way to test students' knowledge.

• *Written reports.* This is another writing assignment that is more formal than journal entries or response logs. Written reports assess students' ability to formulate and organize the information they have found.

• *Group projects.* Peer interaction and the ability to work well with others are important aspects of learning. Group projects help students learn how to integrate information and work with others toward a common goal.

• *Performance assessments.* These assessments are typically done in October and April to show growth over time.

• *Student questions.* We can assess a lot from students by the questions they ask. The secret is allowing students to ask questions about whatever they wonder about, whatever confuses them, what interests them most—not just questions about how to do the assignment. Students are full of wonder and ideas. It is up to teachers to unleash the full power of these questions, for they propel students toward knowledge.

• *Student observations.* Like questions, these can be very informative if we are able to guide students to observe objects related to the conceptual theme.

• *Discussions.* Having students converse with classmates is an easy way to assess their level of understanding and their ideas. Teacher-led discussions yield different information than student-led discussions, so it is constructive to have both.

## Teach for Engagement Rather Than "High-Stakes Tests"

Graduate students of mine, who are also classroom teachers, complain to me all the time that teaching for engagement is not possible because of "high-stakes" testing. Widespread pressure to bring students' reading test scores up dramatically has convinced many teachers that they do not have "time to teach conceptually," mainly because they are worried about end-of-year high-stakes testing. Teachers see evaluation as "either/or": *either* they teach students the methods of high-stakes testing *or* they use alternative forms of assessment, which may cause students to perform more poorly on end-of-level tests because they are not specifically prepped for them. What is the goal of teaching? Is it to test or to help students gain knowledge? Teachers can use a variety of assessments, including norm-referenced tests, to see the "big picture" of their students' abilities. But this does not mean that teachers should give up on improving their instructional practices or on their concern for students' long-term learning habits.

> My students asked questions that led to searching for information and express-ing this knowledge to others. They loved writing reports. I started by having them write a group report using one book in their crate. Eventually I had them do individual reports that were much more in-depth. They were evaluated in simi-lar ways. Everyone in the group got the same grade. Group grades relied heavily on the group's presentation. If we could hear and understand them and if they could answer questions about their topic from the rest of the class listening, they all got an "A." I think that grading is really an individual thing. I really wanted my kids to learn, so I was willing to spend a lot of time working with them until they understood. I cared more about their effort and how much they progressed than any "letter grade." Here another group shares their knowledge about torna-does [see Figure 8.1]. The children had so much fun learning, they did report af-ter report.

Ironically, research has shown that teaching students to become engaged read-ers and to see how much fun learning can be is the best way to increase their test

**FIGURE 8.1.** A group of students sharing their knowledge about tornadoes in a class poster presentation.

scores. Teachers who teach conceptually, implementing the principles discussed in this book, create knowledgeable, sociable, intrinsically motivated students who have choices, feel control over their learning, feel supported by their teacher and peers, and have the competence to put forth the effort needed to be successful. These students do well on their end-of-level tests because they know how to *learn*, not because they know how to *test*. The classroom environment that Margaret and CORI teachers create is supportive and values learning. Students perform better because they are not feeling pressure themselves. Plus, they love to learn, so they read more and then they know more.

The paradox comes when we compare this new evaluation for engagement to current "standards-based" assessments that drive instruction in an opposite direction. The two engagement principles of goals and evaluation are intertwined through all the other CORI principles in some way or another. When teachers implement CORI principles for engagement, including evaluation, they notice a definite difference in their students' attitudes about school as well as their progress and achievement (Guthrie et al., 2000).

## What Does Evaluation Look Like in the Classroom?

Improving test scores happens when we create engaged readers and learners. But, for this to happen, we have to give up some ideas about assessment that research has shown are misleading. Students must be assessed in multiple ways throughout the year to get a clear picture of their progress and achievement.

> I assessed my students in several ways and these evolved over the year. One of my goals was to help my struggling and unmotivated readers to improve. I had such a diverse group of students in terms of their ability that at first I was overwhelmed. As I implemented CORI for my butterfly unit in the fall, I made an effort to build students' background knowledge and teach strategies for reading. I began giving students choices about what to study. I helped students learn how to access books so they could be successful. This made a huge difference! Eventually, my lowest readers could gain information from books by looking at pictures and using other text structures, which gave them confidence. These students could write small paragraphs about their topics. By the time I got to my weather unit, the students had already had success writing reports and using strategies. I used assessments for different reasons. Mainly I wanted to build competence and give my students multiple opportunities to feel successful and believe in themselves.

Evaluation can take several forms in the classroom, depending on the purpose of the assessment. Several of these assessments can feature letter grades, while others may be done to assess student knowledge to guide teacher instruction. Some forms of evaluation can be done daily and weekly, while others may take a week to complete and might be done monthly or quarterly. Finally, some assessments are culminating and are done at the end of each grading period, at the end of a unit, or at the end of the school year. Here are some suggestions.

### Daily or Weekly Assessments

- Observations
- Questions
- Writing assignments
- Journals and reader responses
- Discussions
- Strategy application

### Monthly Assessments

- Reports
- Group or team projects
- Charts, dioramas, posters
- Art projects
- Plus any of the assessments mentioned above

### Culminating or End-of-Unit Assessments

- Video presentations
- Group or team projects
- Plays or dramas

### End-of-Year Assessments

- Portfolio assessments
- Performance assessments

Anything students do in the "Communicate to Others" phase of CORI has the potential to be a graded assignment or project or used for assessing understanding. In Margaret's classroom her students chose from a list of possible options for reports or projects. Some teachers show students how to use a particular strategy, such as finding the main idea on a page, and then practice this strategy over a week or two. Once students illustrate their competence independently through reading the page and writing the main idea, the teacher may give the class a copy of a page from a new, previously unseen book on an unrelated topic. Then the teacher has the class find the main idea on the page and write it in their journals. This activity serves as an assessment to inform the teacher of students' ability to transfer this skill of finding the main idea to another text. From this activity the teacher knows how to move forward, or back, with her instruction.

In CORI classrooms portfolios are the most common way of assessing student progress over time. At the end of the year, students have a meaningful and practical way of seeing their improvement and celebrating their success. Students always collect their best work to show progress over time. The following are some portfolio guidelines for teachers.

## Student Portfolio Guidelines

The purpose of the portfolio is to collect and organize students' work that occurs as part of the Concept-Oriented Reading Instruction. Teachers may use portfolios to monitor students' educational growth and to communicate progress to administrators, parents, and educators. Students' work should illustrate their interests and motivations as well as their cognitive abilities. Portfolios demonstrate that students are active, productive, and strategic in observing phenomena and in searching for, comprehending, and communicating information or knowledge.

Every student will develop a portfolio of his or her work during the course of the academic year. Student portfolios will be contained within a spiral notebook, accordion folder, or other means of collecting and organizing student work. Visible at the beginning of the portfolio will be a table of contents, *prepared by students*, containing the items in each section of the portfolio.

Portfolios will be divided into eight sections:

1. Table of Contents
2. Records of Observing and Searching
3. Themes and Summaries
4. Applications and Extensions (of the knowledge to new problems)
5. Book Logs
6. My Personal Favorites
7. Letters Home
8. Optional Items

The following descriptions may be used for sections of student portfolios.

*Table of Contents.* Students will make a title for each piece entered in the portfolio, placing the item in its proper order in the table of contents. Dates, sections, or categories may organize the table of contents.

*Records of Observing and Searching.* These records may include descriptions of what students have observed in "real-world" science (or social studies) activities and what they found personally interesting. This section may include drawings and sketches, concept maps of what is being learned, notes, and outlines. The term "real-world" means that students observe actual objects, such as the moon, birds, flowers, clouds, or fossils, rather than photographs or writings about them. The written descriptions do not attempt to be "scientific" explanations, but rather statements about "what is there." Such resources as books, references, explanations or directions to follow for experiments or demonstrations, and illustrations that have been located in search activities should be included. Students may also include charts, diagrams, signs, journals, and notes taken during their reading of informational books.

*Themes and Summaries*. Interpretations of the main themes of novels, chapters of narrative books, folk tales, and literary materials are included. Thematic statements contain students' perceptions and judgments of the main themes of literary works, with support from the plot, characters, symbolism, and other literary features. Texts may be read both in the classroom and at home. The writing may be informed by group discussion, but it will be the students' own work. Each student will further explore the story or book by writing one of the following:

A study (account or description) of one of the characters.
A written statement of imagery in the narrative.
A timeline of events in the text.
A personal response to the materials that expresses the student's own experiences in reading it.

*Informational* texts that are especially interesting and important to the student may also be summarized. Most of the texts should be student-selected. Informational texts may be represented through student-authored informational booklets, physical models, book reviews, video documentaries, simulations, and by other means. On a few occasions the teacher will assign the same text to be summarized by all the students, for purposes of checking comprehension and comparing the students to one another. Students should synthesize multiple texts and sources including the illustrations, diagrams, maps, and charts, explaining key concepts such as the weather, pollution, adaptation to the environment, or energy cycles. Students' scientific concepts and principles should address questions such as "How do the seasons affect the growth of plants and animals?" or "How does the water cycle (snow or precipitation, formation of rivers) influence the weather patterns in different parts of the world at the same time?"

*Applications and Extensions*. As students apply their conceptual knowledge to solve new problems, the applications will be placed in the portfolio. Applications may include written statements, informational stories, physical models such as a shoe-box-sized diorama, or documents such as illustrations or charts.

*Book Logs*. Students will maintain a log of the books they read, inside and outside of school. The logs will contain a section for literary texts and another for informational books and references. Students may write book reviews and enter them into their book log section. The book reviews may be simple statements of "Why I chose this book" or an extended critique of the strengths and weaknesses of all aspects of the book.

*My Personal Favorites*. In this section students choose their favorite work. They might include a report, illustration, chart, story, or other expression of their conceptual understanding or writing. This does not have to represent their "best" accomplishment, but is should be an example of an activity they thoroughly enjoyed.

*Letters Home*. At least one time per month, and possibly once a week, students will compose a letter to family members at home. The letter will be a communication of what students are learning. It may reference new concepts (what the student is learning about, such as hurricanes) or new strategies (what the student is learning how to do, such as how to find books or how to take notes). Family members may be invited to reply by indicating how they think students are doing recently in reading and science (or social studies).

*Optional Items*. Both students and teachers may add any material to this open-ended section.

## Performance Assessments

The purpose of performance assessments is to test students' conceptual knowledge and their ability to use strategies in gaining this knowledge. Typically performance assessments last for 1 week and are administered in October and April. Performance assessments show growth over time, with the four parts of the assessment epitomizing the four phases of CORI. Throughout the year, as students become familiar with the phases of CORI and get used to using the strategies for learning that are associated with each phase, learning becomes easier for them. By April most students can apply their knowledge about learning to any topic.

The performance assessment usually begins on a Monday and lasts until Friday. Students work on their assessment materials for 1 hour a day. This works best if it is the first hour of the day so that their minds are relatively clear. During this testing week students are not allowed to gather information from other sources than the ones provided in class. The different parts of the performance assessment are described next. Examples of an actual performance assessment are shown in Appendix B, including a scoring rubric.

*Prior-Knowledge Assessment*. The first portion of the assessment focuses on finding out what students know about a topic they will be studying during the next week. For example, let us say this performance assessment is on life cycles. Think of a broad conceptual question that the students can answer over a week's time, serving as the focus of the assessment for the entire week. The question is best if it compares two aspects of, or possibilities within, the same concept. For example, students might write the answer to the following question on life cycles: EXPLAIN HOW CRABS AND TURTLES LIVE AND GROW. In writing your answer, you may want to think about the following questions to help you. How are they similar? How are they different from each other? How do they live and survive in their habitat?"

This first portion is given on Monday morning and takes the students about 20 minutes. Since this is not a topic that has been covered yet, they may or may not have much knowledge about it.

*Observation Log.* The second portion of the assessment involves students observing and recording their observations. This part also involves searching for information about the topic and keeping a record of what is found. The goal for students is to find as much information as possible that helps them answer the question. The observation log has a page for drawing and labeling what they see. The second page is for writing down what they see and describing it in detail. The third page is for writing down questions they may have while observing and for recording any changes they see over time.

*Writing Log for the Search.* The next portion of the log is for writing and recording the information that students find in their search for information. The pages are for students to record the information they are gathering from books and other sources. This writing log asks students to record where they find their information (e.g., the name of the book), their notes from reading, and what they are learning.

| Date | Book title or source | What information are you finding? | What are you learning? |
|------|---------------------|----------------------------------|------------------------|
|      |                     |                                  |                        |
|      |                     |                                  |                        |

The search portion of the assessment lasts for almost 4 days. Books and other source materials must be available for the students to use during this time. If you do not have enough books for the assessment, interlibrary loans can help immensely. Borrowing sets of books from the library works great for this 1-week assessment. On Monday students will not have the full day available for searching because of the prior-knowledge assessment. Students may use additional pages for their observation log, if they are needed. The students should be encouraged to find as much information as possible to answer the question.

*Conceptual Knowledge Assessment.* On Friday students complete the final assessment for the week. The conceptual knowledge assessment asks that students explain their knowledge through a combination of drawing and writing. Students may *not* use their notes from the week's worth of information gathering. First, students draw a picture to show how crabs and turtles live and grow. Next, they write an explanation of how crabs and turtles live and grow. They may use their drawing to help them with their written explanation. Combining drawing and writing allows fairness for the students who may not be as adept with their writing. Conversely, some students may be less able to explain their knowledge through drawing and may do better with the written portion.

*Knowledge Transfer.* The final portion of the assessment is a question that asks students to apply what they know about crabs and turtles to a different situation. This is a hypothetical question and is a *completely optional* question for the performance assessment. Older students do better on this portion because it is easier for them, developmentally, to think in abstract and hypothetical terms. For younger students, this portion of the assessment is not necessary. An example of a transfer question for the assessment on crabs and turtles might be the following: "Given what you have learned about how crabs and turtles live and grow, think of what might happen in the following situation. What if all the water in the ocean dried up for 3 days. What would happen?"

This question requires that students think about a drastic (albeit temporary) situation that would affect the life cycle of these animals. If students have conceptual knowledge of these animals, they will understand how to transfer their knowledge. Typically, in younger grades students have a difficult time with a drastic situation lasting only for 3 days. Hypothetical situations are more appropriate for upper-grade students.

A scoring rubric is included with the examples of all portions of the performance assessment in Appendix B. The scoring rubric has up to nine levels that may easily be converted to letter grades. Performance assessments are easy to administer and time-consuming to grade, but they provide teachers with an accurate picture of what students can and cannot do. In April, the performance assessment is important for students if CORI has been taught all year. Students love the performance assessment because it is what they are used to doing. Most students see it as just another project rather than a "test." It is a valuable way for teachers to measure conceptual knowledge growth. It is so validating and exciting to see that you have taught students how to be lifelong learners.

An optional assessment may be made by giving students the Motivations for Reading Questionnaire (MRQ) (Wigfield, Guthrie, & McGough, 1996) early in the year and again at the end of the year to see if their motivations have changed. Appendix E shows the MRQ divided into the two basic categories of "intrinsic" motivations and "extrinsic" motivations. To administer this assessment, you will need to have the statements ordered on the page in *random* order, not grouped by category or category headings. Leave a space by each statement, so the students can rate each question on a scale of 1 to 4 of how true the statement is for them. Although you will probably not be running correlation statistics on the students' answers, you will be able to see what kinds of factors motivate your students to learn, which is exciting information to have. If anything, the information gleaned from this questionnaire may help you to pay closer attention to your *purposes* for your lessons and activities. This information might even help your expectations to rise, which adds challenge and motivation to your lessons.

Through administering this questionnaire in two separate studies (see Wigfield, 1997), Alan Wigfield and his colleagues drew three conclusions. First, the categories of motivations were related, which means that children do not read *only* for intrinsic or extrinsic reasons. Second, the children who are motivated to read for numerous reasons do not want to avoid books or tasks that challenge or are difficult for them. Finally, there is a positive relationship between competition and work avoidance, which indicates that teachers should be careful about reading activities that promote competition.

There are several different kinds of motivations for reading that have been measured reliably. Several researchers claim that the declines in motivation we see as children progress through school are due to classroom environments and changes that occur in schools (Eccles, Wigfield, Midgley, et al., 1993; Oldfather & McLaughlin, 1993). These researchers found that the classroom environment and the school itself can greatly affect students' motivation to learn. Such aspects of schooling as large-group organization, the lack of student choice or decision-making ability, how positive and personal (or not) the teacher is with her students, and how much teacher control and discipline are emphasized can contribute to students' believing that they are not competent or skilled readers. In addition, these factors create an environment where grades and rewards are more important than learning, curiosity, and involvement (Wigfield, 1997).

## How Can Teachers Implement Evaluation in Their Classrooms?

Assessment that is varied and frequent provides teachers with a more realistic view of how students are progressing in school. When teachers assess students continually through observation, running records, authentic tasks, writing, discussion, and the various other ways already cited, teachers can hone their teaching to meet the diverse needs of their students. School can become more meaningful and fun. Lucy Calkins (1997) believes that the assessments we give should push us, as teachers, to look at all our students and their various strengths, and then to look closely at ourselves and our own work. Calkins counsels teachers to consider the range of developmental abilities already evident within our classroom and then to design a curriculum that meets all our students where they are currently and takes each student a level higher, instead of teaching to the whole class or to the so-called average student.

Within each classroom, teachers can begin to implement evaluation in a way that benefits both student and teacher. The crucial connection between assessment, curriculum, and instruction must be made if we are to engage our students not only in learning to read but also in reading to learn. Assessments must have a *purpose* and be able to give us information about our students that we, as teachers, can use to help them progress. Assessment does not have to be a "twice a year" battle of time and wits. Having a variety of ways to assess students enables teachers to appreciate them as truly literate people.

Children should immediately and consistently sense their teacher's interest in the wholeness of each of them as readers. We must teach in ways that help students realize that reading is more than mere words on a page, but rather a way of living our lives (Calkins, 1997). Reading informs us, challenges us, teaches us, and entertains us. The demand for literacy these days is so high in part because information is growing at an exponential rate. We must teach our students to read to learn and to read to live more fully because they must depend heavily on these skills to be successful in their lives—*outside* of school as well as inside the classroom. Engagement in reading occurs on several levels. Our ability to assess our students allows us to teach them at their present level and holds our teaching accountable if there is no progress. Highly related to evaluation is how we reward and praise students. What are the best ways to help our students succeed?

## PRINCIPLE 9 OF COHERENT INSTRUCTION: REWARDS AND PRAISE

The concluding CORI principle is "Rewards and Praise." Rewards and praise are connected to evaluation in several ways. Often teachers reward students with grades based on incentive programs. A close and careful look at rewards and praise is important in a classroom where teachers are striving to engage students. Implementing an extrinsic incentive program that undermines the natural, intrinsic motivation the foregoing CORI principles work to create can ruin the application of several principles of engagement. A balance must be struck between grades, rewards, incentives, and praise to sustain students whose goal primarily should be *to learn*.

### What Do I Mean by Rewards and Praise?

Rewards may be tangible or intangible. Tangible rewards may include stickers, candy, points in a contest, marbles in a jar, recognition on a public chart, money, pizza parties, or gold stars. Intangible rewards come chiefly in the form of teacher praise and feedback.

Think back to the vignette about Margaret's students waiting outside at the Delta Center for the ice skating event. The students' spontaneous excitement about snowflakes did not derive from candy bars, stickers on a poster, or points in a contest. *The reward was the learning itself*, the knowledge, the wonder, and curiosity about snowflakes. In fact, the only time Margaret used a "treat" in her classroom was to celebrate someone's birthday. If Margaret brought a treat to school, everyone got one; the treat was never made contingent on a specific behavior or success-ful competition.

> The kids in my class got so into weather they would ask if they could stay in for recess to keep working. If students had books and papers spread out on the floor, they didn't want to disturb the materials (i.e., clean it up) to go to recess or lunch. "Please, Mrs. Barnes, can we come back to the room after lunch so we can keep working on our posters?" I loved how excited they were because it made school so much fun for me. I watched students work for weeks on a re-port, and then the time came to present it to the class. The shocking thing was after everyone had finished their presentations, they all wanted to do another one! Once they had written a report on tornadoes, they wanted to study floods. They thought of things to study about weather that hadn't even occurred to me. The excitement of a candy bar never would have lasted as long as the fun my students had just reading and learning about the weather.

## What Do Rewards and Praise Look Like in a Classroom?

There are several incentive programs in schools to get students to read. In fact, most elementary teachers commonly use some sort of reading incentive program in their classrooms (Moore & Fawson, 1992). Abundant evidence also supports the opinion that giving rewards and positive incentives for book reading increases the time and effort expended in book reading activities (Gambrell & Marinak, 1997). Many administrators and teachers believe that simply giving praise, candy, stickers, gold stars, or points in a contest will increase students' motivation to read. Inter-estingly, intermediate-grade students do not consider rewards and incentives to read important (Worthy, 2000). In fact, Kohn (1993) found that when points and other incentives for reading are offered, students get the impression that reading is a chore rather than the goal. They begin to think reading is valuable only when a reward is given for doing it (see Worthy, 2002). Students' motivation to read is thereby undermined. But rewards and incentives are more complicated than an "all or nothing" approach.

In the short run, rewards can increase students' attention regarding specific ac-tivities, but when extrinsic rewards and incentives dominate the classroom envi-ronment, students' focus comes to center more on performance than on learning (Flink, Boggianno, Main, Barrett, & Katz, 1992; see also Guthrie, Cox, et al., 2000). When students become too performance-oriented, they care more about getting the right answer, finishing assignments first, and getting high grades than they do on understanding what they read, learning valuable reading strategies, reading for enjoyment, or learning about content.

Deborah Stipek and Kathy Seal tell a story in their book *Motivated Minds: Raising Children to Love Learning* (2001) that illustrates what happens when our goals are only extrinsic. The story was about a man who was bothered by some loud neighborhood boys screaming and laughing as they played outside near his home. He was convinced they were doing it deliberately to annoy him. He decided to go outside and tell the boys that he would pay them each a quarter to scream and carry on. They boys were thrilled to get paid for doing something they loved to do anyway. After they were finished playing, the man gave them each a quarter. The next day, the boys came back to make their noise. This time, the man told them he could pay them only 20 cents, but they were still happy enough to take the money; they figured 20 cents was better than nothing. The next day, the boys came back again to play and make noise. This time, the man told the boys he was getting low on change and could only afford to pay them a dime. The boys decided a dime was still better than nothing and accepted his offer. The next day, the boys came back. They screamed and carried on, and when they were finished playing, the man came out and told them he was out of money and could no longer pay them. Frustrated and angry, the boys left. They were not going to play, scream, and carry on for nothing! The boys' goal had shifted to the reward and not the fun. Once the money ran out, playing seemed not so much fun anymore because all the kids came to care about was how much money they could get. This is how extrinsic rewards often subvert their intended aims.

When students are focused on extrinsic rewards, their focus is not on learning. Students whose chief focus is on the reward end up relying on surface-level strategies such as memorization, guessing, using "Cliff Notes," and even resorting to cheating to get the assignment done or to get the right answer. The reward becomes the goal, rather than learning or reading itself. These same students tend to avoid challenge and give up easily when they are frustrated (Guthrie, Cox, et al., 2000). Over time, extrinsic rewards can undermine a student's intrinsic motivation to read and learn, which can affect an entire classroom of learners (Guthrie, Cox, et al., 2000).

Rewards and praise do have their place, but they are most effective when they do not dominate classroom proceedings. If teachers wholly rely on rewards other than praise, students become extrinsically motivated and achievement decreases. Effective teachers consistently provide informative feedback in the form of compliments that help students feel appreciated. Compliments can also help students feel pride and a sense of accomplishment in their work (Guthrie, Cox, et al., 2000). Praise works in classrooms when it is given appropriately and sincerely. It should be contingent upon effort and achievement. Students should be praised who work hard in the face of difficulty and do a good job. Praise should also be *specific to the particulars* of the accomplishment; after all, hearing "good job" or "nice work" all the time loses its power and punch after a while. It is far more motivating to say things such as "You really found interesting facts about hurricanes in your report" or "I never knew that tsunamis and hurricanes had so many differing characteristics." Praise is also effective when it is spontaneous, helps students to appreciate their own work and contribution, attributes success to the amount of effort involved in doing the assignment well, and fosters an appreciation for the strategies it took to complete the assignment (Brophy, 1981; Guthrie, Cox, et al., 2000).

## How Do Teachers Implement Rewards and Praise in Their Classrooms?

Wlodkowski (1985) suggested that praise should be specific, sincere, and sufficient. Praise should also be properly given for success that is praiseworthy in the manner that is preferred by the student. This is the "3S–3P" formula for praise. This method makes sense because students readily sense when the praise given is not sincere or meaningful. Praise is not efficacious when students feel manipulated or controlled (Flink et al., 1992).

More than a decade ago, when I was a classroom teacher of fifth graders, I remember taking a classroom management class that taught us how to control our students' behavior. We were taught to put marbles in a jar when our students were behaving appropriately, and they would continue to as well. The idea was for the students to behave so well for so long that the jar would fill up with marbles, at which point the students would get pizza for lunch, or a longer recess, or some other reward. We were also taught that if students' behavior got out of hand we could control it by taking a couple of marbles out of the jar, thereby punishing the students.

Being a new teacher, naturally I tried this. The problem was that I added marbles all the time, but I kept forgetting to ever take marbles out! I liked the classroom noisy and the students talking and working together. One day a student who had been fighting at recess with another student came into class after recess and knocked over a desk, disturbing the entire class. It occurred to me that taking a big fistful of marbles out of the jar would not punish this student for knocking over the desk so much as it would punish the entire class; marbles would not solve his behavior problem.

I learned quickly that engagement in school had nothing to do with marbles in a jar. I could not manipulate my students by trying to control their behavior. Intuitively I knew that I needed to engage their minds in meaningful learning. So, the marble jar did not last. Oh, I wish I knew then what I know now about intrinsic motivation! And yet, when I visit schools, I still see management systems like this in place. Praise and rewards cannot be about controlling students' behavior or making them "feel good." Teachers need to build competence, autonomy, and a sense of belonging. Praise must be about appreciating and celebrating the success our students have as learners and readers. I believe there is enough knowledge to go around. When we are working in our classrooms to help our students succeed and *progress* as learners, then every student can win, not just the students who finish first or who get the "A" grade. Effort and persistence are valued right along with learning. Ironically, when students have the tools and strategies to be in control of their own learning, they become engaged in learning. With experience, teachers create this engagement through a balanced contribution of autonomy and support, real-world interaction, collaboration, and other processes, in addition to rewards and praise.

My grading system was not traditional. My focus was on learning and allowing students to become independent thinkers, readers, and writers. The letter grade did not matter to me. I worked with my students to help them with what they needed to be successful. I looked at each student individually. I compared their individual progress *over time*, not to other students in the class. This attitude kept the students free to learn because they weren't worried about grades or pressure. The students kept writing folders, and I used them to conference with my students and help them monitor their progress. Each student had a file in which to keep reports and important assignments or projects.

I remember one student who came into my class in about October from another school. He had obviously been in a classroom where he was rewarded constantly for everything he did. One day I asked the students to write something we were studying in our butterfly unit. This boy asked me, "What will we get?" I remember being caught off guard because my students never asked me that. I looked at him and I said, "You get *smart*! In my class you get smart." He never asked again after that.

I kept portfolios as my main assessment. I would collect students' best work, and they would help me decide what projects or assignments should go into the portfolios. At parent–teacher conferences I showed the parents their child's work and how much he or she had progressed over time. We talked about the different things we studied and the future projects that were planned. I told the parents how much effort their child exerted (or not), if they challenged themselves, or improved, and how. As the parents were leaving, I'd say, "Oh, by the way, here is your child's report card." Grades were not my focus. I taught my students how to learn. They became lifelong learners. They loved school. They loved reading and writing. That was the most important thing to me. CORI changed me and the way I looked at grading.

I know there are many teachers like Margaret who *do* emphasize learning and let the grades follow. Teaching within the CORI framework, with these principles in place, helps teachers empower their students to read to learn. CORI students read to learn because gaining knowledge becomes their purpose and goal. Many of my graduate students, who are practicing teachers, say they would love to teach this way, but "what do I tell my principal?" I know that most teachers, administrators, and many parents focus primarily on grades. Now more than ever, it seems to me that grades are the focus. But I believe they should be a measure of what students have in fact *learned*, as opposed to how they have *performed*, although I realize that often these two go hand in hand. I just like to imagine how things would be if the focus were on the actual learning and knowledge and the process of getting there—rather than on the grade. Were that to happen, I believe, there would be a lot more interest in the weather.

# CHAPTER 9

## Why Teach This Way?

### WHAT ARE THE BENEFITS OF CORI?

Research has been conducted on CORI classrooms since CORI's conception in 1994. Early research conducted on CORI classrooms showed that the effects this instruction had on students' motivation and conceptual knowledge was significant, compared to traditional methods of reading instruction. Students in 10 classrooms within three schools were involved in a 3-year study. Half of these classrooms featured CORI.

For example, researchers interviewed students and asked them about CORI activities. In addition, both CORI and traditional students in the study participated in a 1-week performance assessment to test their ability to search for information about ponds and deserts. The goal of the assessment was for students to gain as much knowledge as possible about ponds and deserts in 1 week. Students in CORI classrooms were significantly higher on measures of motivation, strategies for searching for information, and conceptual knowledge than students in traditional classrooms. This was true for both third- and fifth-grade students, even after students' prior knowledge about the topic and reading levels were accounted for at the beginning of the year.

When comparisons were made across grade levels, results showed that the third-grade CORI students exceeded the fifth-grade students in the traditional classrooms in terms of motivated strategy use. This was also true for measures of conceptual knowledge. So, the third-grade CORI students were more engaged and gained higher levels of conceptual knowledge (about ponds and deserts) than both the third-grade and fifth-grade students in traditional reading classrooms (Guthrie, Van Meter, et al., 1996, 1998).

One of the best features of CORI is that it is a framework for organizing and integrating literacy processes with content knowledge. There is no prepackaged way to teach. Teaching CORI is flexible—as long as all of the principles are in place. This is both exciting and daunting, depending on the teacher. I like to think of CORI classrooms as comparable to the weather quilt: if every square were exactly the same, the quilt would not be very dynamic. Instead, every teacher brings her strengths and experience to this framework, making each classroom with CORI instruction look a little different. One teacher may emphasize one principle, such as autonomy support, because she is comfortable allowing students to self-direct themselves as they learn. Another teacher may be especially good at explicit strategy instruction and finding incredibly interesting books. As long as all the principles are included over the 12-week theme, students will be engaged. The idea is not to reinvent the wheel (or have every quilt look the same) but to rethink how instruction is organized and tied together to bring more coherence to the teaching of the reading process and to learning and fully comprehending written content.

## SOME FREQUENTLY ASKED QUESTIONS

### How Do the Four Phases of CORI Work?

The four phases are not exactly static. This means that you don't typically do Observe and Personalize activities and then stop completely and go on to Search and Retrieve. Often two or three of these phases can be touched on in one CORI instructional period or at least during the same week. The goal of the various phases is to help you plan from week to week and to make sure that the instruction covers these areas fairly completely over time.

The goals for Observe and Personalize are different than those for Communicate to Others. The four Phases of CORI help you organize your instruction to: (1) engage students and create interest in your content area in a variety of ways; (2) teach valuable strategies for finding and accessing different kinds of information; (3) teach valuable strategies for creating or extracting meaning from the information gathered or read (for example, in a narrative work); and (4) teach students ways to communicate this information to a real audience. Such *principles of CORI* as real-world observation, interesting texts, and strategy instruction will cross over and blend into one another during several phases. The phases are there to keep your instruction focused on your reading process goals and your content goals in order to maximize learning.

Figure 9.1 illustrates how teachers can focus their instruction during a typical 12-week unit. This graph depicts the phases as fairly static, but the instruction would just *emphasize one phase over the others* while students are either observing, gathering information, reading for understanding, and then communicating to others. Remember that students will be communicating their knowledge as they observe. They will also comprehend the information they observe to be able to represent it in a graph, just as Brooke did with the temperature graph for January (see Chapter 3). One of the most important things is to remain flexible. Once your stu-

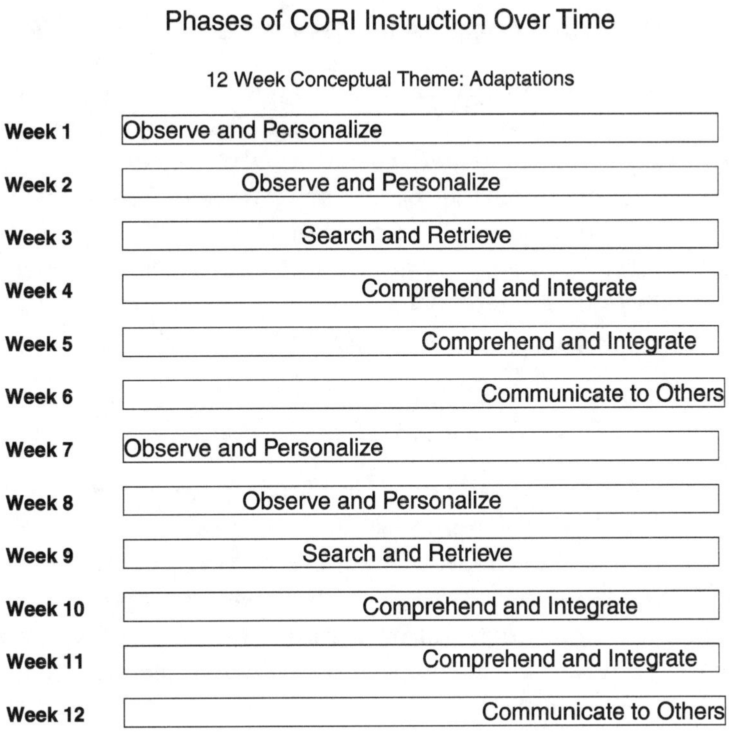

## Phases of CORI Instruction Over Time

### 12 Week Conceptual Theme: Adaptations

| | |
|---|---|
| Week 1 | Observe and Personalize |
| Week 2 | Observe and Personalize |
| Week 3 | Search and Retrieve |
| Week 4 | Comprehend and Integrate |
| Week 5 | Comprehend and Integrate |
| Week 6 | Communicate to Others |
| Week 7 | Observe and Personalize |
| Week 8 | Observe and Personalize |
| Week 9 | Search and Retrieve |
| Week 10 | Comprehend and Integrate |
| Week 11 | Comprehend and Integrate |
| Week 12 | Communicate to Others |

**FIGURE 9.1.** Phases of CORI over time.

dents get "turned on" to the weather, the first 14 Amendments to the U.S. Constitution, the U.S. Civil War, mammals and reptiles, the systems of the human body, or whatever your conceptual theme happens to be, they will begin to influence the direction your instruction takes.

## How Much Time Does It Take to Prepare a Unit?

There is a front-end investment that teachers must make to organize their instruction for a CORI unit. If you follow the outline presented in the "Building a CORI Unit" sections of this volume, you will have most of the work done. The following chapters have a "Building a CORI Unit" section in them: Chapter 2 (Choosing a Conceptual Theme), Chapter 3 (Observe and Personalize), Chapter 4 (Search and Retrieve), Chapter 5 (Comprehend and Integrate), and Chapter 7 (Communicate to Others). Choose your theme, and then begin with your goals for each phase. Once you have your Instructional Planning Charts filled out for each phase, you can then think of materials or lessons you have already used that would fit into this framework. For most teachers, that is an empowering feeling; they think of lesson after lesson that they can teach in a new way.

## How Do I Teach CORI Principles If I Use a Basal Reading Program?

Once you have filled out the Reading and Content Goals, Student Activities, and the Teaching Procedures on the four Instructional Planning Charts, you are ready to think about books, stories, materials, and resources that you can use to meet your goals. Look through the basal reading program, and find the stories that will fit best into your framework. Use it as a resource. Teach the stories when they fit into your framework, not the other way around. You will have a much more difficult time fitting the CORI framework into your basal program than you will finding great literature and activities to fit into a CORI framework.

## What If I Am the Only One at My School Who Teaches CORI?

CORI takes teacher collaboration and support along with the principal's support, to be really successful. That is not to say that you cannot teach it by yourself; of course, you can. But, in the schools where there are several CORI teachers, there is also a great additional resource. Teachers in the same grade levels or who are close friends find that teaching with CORI principles is much easier with a friend. You will find that if several teachers in your school begin to implement CORI principles, you will work with one another to try new activities, use one another as literary resources, and trade units with each other halfway through the year. The same principles of collaboration that we espouse for students also work equally well for teachers. Two heads are better than one when it comes to planning, organizing, sharing ideas, and coaching each other to help your students become successful learners.

There were only two or three CORI teachers in each school when we began our CORI implementation and research in Maryland. We compared CORI teachers to traditional teachers. What we found was that by the time the research project ended, 4 years later, the traditional teachers had already begun to implement some CORI principles. Once the research was published, these teachers and others implemented all the CORI principles.

## How Do I Explain CORI to Concerned Parents?

I know of CORI teachers who teach in a school where the students have been completely unengaged in school. One teacher, in particular, complained that before CORI she could not think of anything to get the students engaged in school or to get the parents' support in helping her do so.

After learning about CORI in one of my classes, she decided to begin a CORI unit immediately, in the middle of the year, on civil rights. She had a racially diverse class, so she decided to allow her students the choice of learning about African Americans, Mexican Americans, Native Americans, and women. As the teacher, she would model her instruction as she undertook to explain the civil rights of Japanese Americans.

Her goal was to help her students make connections between what civil rights means to these groups and what civil rights means to individuals personally. I remember her telling me that her students were so engaged that they came to school when classes were canceled for parent–teacher conferences just to work on their reports and research in the library. In fact, this school typically has a very low turnout for parent–teacher conferences, as it is. She said she has never had so many parents attend conferences; they all wanted to know what she was doing to make their kids want to come to school on their day off! Now, that is engagement!

This instruction got not only the parents' attention but also that of several other teachers in the school. Now there are many teachers in the school teaching CORI principles and making a difference for their students; it is amazing! So, if you have parents who do not seem concerned, give them time. If you have parents who are concerned and involved, great!

## Is CORI Only for Upper-Grade Students?

CORI is *not* only for upper-grade students. Teaching children to think, question, and explore various types of text, to understand what they read, to work well with others, and to understand science, social studies, or other content area concepts in a meaningful way can take place at any age. I have been in first-grade classrooms where the teacher taught the life cycle by observing eggs incubate over time and eventually hatch into chicks. These young children read all kinds of expository books about chickens and eggs, how things grow, and the parts of a chicken, as well as narrative stories about birds and other animals. Although these young children were just learning to read and write, they were taught from the very beginning how to be strategic in their thinking and how to make sense of the world around them.

We did research in CORI classrooms in grades 3 through 5. Currently CORI is being implemented in all grade levels in several states. Since I have been teaching college students about CORI, I have had students in Utah implement CORI units in grades pre-K through advanced-placement high school history classes. Although research has not been conducted in secondary, advanced placement, or pre-K through second grade classrooms, many of them are like Margaret's class. As a teacher, the CORI principles made sense to her and validated several of the principles she was currently using in her classroom. Learning about the CORI principles augmented what she was already doing and helped her reorganize her instruction to provide the structure she needed. I am currently working with teachers in secondary schools who have implemented CORI at that level. It will work with *any* grade level—it just looks different. You need to adjust the principles to meet the needs of your students in terms of texts, strategies, concepts, and so on. I teach CORI principles in all of my college courses, and they are transferable among all grade levels.

## Will CORI Work with Diverse Groups of Students?

CORI principles are intended to accommodate all types and categories of students. In fact, many principles bridge the gap for all students—*everyone* can succeed. The ability to think and learn is universal. Students with learning disabilities, those who speak English as a second language, and those who have other challenges can all participate in all aspects of CORI. Some consideration, though, needs to be given to building appropriate background knowledge or in helping students who may not be familiar with particular themes and concepts.

All students can get excited about observing snowflakes. Students of different ability levels, ones who speak other languages, or students who have never experienced snow can all participate in observational activities such as this.

Students can interact socially in numerous ways. As Margaret observed, her struggling readers loved to work on team or group reports with better readers because the peer interaction helped *both* students. Providing students with opportunities to work together on projects, reports, observations, and making charts or posters can and should include everyone.

Book selection is another way that everyone can learn and participate. Teachers must select text levels that are appropriate for the student population. Nonetheless, the books selected should reflect a wide range of reading levels. Choose books that challenge the proficient readers, and choose other books that allow struggling readers to glean information from photographs, illustrations, diagrams, captions, and more easily understandable text. Strategy instruction is also important with diverse groups. One of the most significant features of CORI is that it teaches students how to understand and access information.

Students who are often "pulled out" of the classroom for special services such as reading intervention, speech therapy, and so on, need the coherence that CORI brings to the classroom. These students have a hard enough time feeling connected to the other students in the class. CORI can help build that coherence for them. Including these students in the activities and projects is an opportunity to increase these students' need for competence, belonging, and autonomy. CORI teachers have commented that this instruction has motivated the unmotivated and has made even the lowest-achieving students progress the most (Guthrie & Cox, 1998).

## CONCLUDING THOUGHTS

I believe that there are many ways to teach a child to read. I do not believe in a silver bullet or in a quick fix. I can say that I do believe in teachers. I believe in their knowledge, expertise, and their ability to make everyday events seem extraordinary. CORI is a framework in which teachers can organize their own instruction in their own way to meet the three basic needs that *all* children have to be self-regulated, self-motivated students: competence, a sense of belonging, and autonomy. The CORI principles satisfy these three needs in numerous ways.

The four phases and nine principles of CORI may seem overwhelming. But, put quite simply, at the heart of CORI are knowledge and the process of how to gain this knowledge. CORI classrooms are classrooms where students are excited about learning. Students are motivated, strategy-oriented, and sociable—that is, they are *engaged*. The result of this kind of instruction is students who are empowered. Students know how to think, question, solve problems, and find answers to any of their questions in the pages of a book or in numerous other ways. Students learn how to learn, and this process can then last for a lifetime.

As teachers, you are able to "light the fire within." What could be better than that?

# APPENDIX A

## Instructional Planning Charts

# INSTRUCTIONAL PLANNING CHART

Conceptual Theme:

Phase 1: Observe and Personalize

| Educational Goals | Student Activities | Teaching Strategies | Materials/ Resources |
|---|---|---|---|
| Reading: | | | |
| Content: | | | |

# INSTRUCTIONAL PLANNING CHART

Conceptual Theme:

Phase 2: Search and Retrieve

| Educational Goals | Student Activities | Teaching Strategies | Materials/ Resources |
|---|---|---|---|
| Reading: | | | |
| Content: | | | |

# INSTRUCTIONAL PLANNING CHART

Conceptual Theme:

Phase 3: Comprehend and Integrate

| Educational Goals | Student Activities | Teaching Strategies | Materials/ Resources |
|---|---|---|---|
| Reading: | | | |
| Content: | | | |

# INSTRUCTIONAL PLANNING CHART

Conceptual Theme:

Phase 4: Communicate to Others

| Educational Goals | Student Activities | Teaching Strategies | Materials/ Resources |
|---|---|---|---|
| Reading: | | | |
| Content: | | | |

# APPENDIX B

## Performance Assessment and Scoring Rubric

### PORTION 1: PRIOR-KNOWLEDGE ASSESSMENT

**Name:** _____   **Date:** _____

In the space below, EXPLAIN HOW CRABS AND TURTLES LIVE AND GROW. In writing your answer, you may want to think about the following questions to help you. How are they similar? How are they different from each other? How do they live and survive in their habitats?

_____

_____

_____

_____

_____

_____

_____

_____

_____

_____

_____

_____

_____

_____

_____

_____

_____

_____

_____

_____

_____

_____

# PORTION 2: OBSERVATION LOG

**Name:**_____  **Date:**_____

**Instructions:** This log is for you to write down the information that you learn this week while you observe crabs and turtles. You will write in the log every day. You may use as many pages as you need. Some of the information available to you during the week will be helpful, and some will not. Remember to choose information that will be the most helpful to you in answering the question below.

**The question you are trying to answer is:** EXPLAIN HOW CRABS AND TURTLES LIVE AND GROW. In thinking and writing your answer, you may want to think about the following questions to help you. What is a crab? What is a turtle? What are their important characteristics? How do they live and survive in their habitats? Answer each part of the Observation Log every day. Write as much as you can.

A.  What are you looking at? Draw and describe what you see.

You may use this page for drawing and labeling what you see.

B. What questions do you have?

_____

_____

_____

_____

_____

_____

_____

_____

_____

_____

_____

_____

_____

_____

_____

_____

_____

_____

_____

_____

_____

_____

_____

_____

_____

_____

_____

_____

_____

_____

_____

_____

_____

_____

C. What are you learning? What is changing or happening?

# PORTION 3: WRITING LOG FOR THE SEARCH

**Name:** _____     **Date:** _____

**Instructions:** This log is for you to write down the information that you learn this week while you read about crabs and turtles. You will write in the log every day. You may use as many pages as you need. When you read, some books will have information that will be helpful to you and some will not. Remember to choose information that will be the most helpful to you in answering the question below.

**The question you are trying to answer is:** EXPLAIN HOW CRABS AND TURTLES LIVE AND GROW. In thinking and writing your answer, you may want to think about the following questions to help you. What is a crab? What is a turtle? What are their important characteristics? How do they live and survive in their habitat?

Answer each part of the Writing Log every day. Be sure to record the books you used to get your information, the kinds of information you gathered, and what you learned from what you read. Write as much as you can.

| Date | Book title or source | What information are you finding? | What are you learning? |
|------|----------------------|-----------------------------------|------------------------|
|      |                      |                                   |                        |

| Date | Book title or source | What information are you finding? | What are you learning? |
| --- | --- | --- | --- |
| | | | |

| Date | Book title or source | What information are you finding? | What are you learning? |
|---|---|---|---|
|  |  |  |  |

## PORTION 4: CONCEPTUAL KNOWLEDGE ASSESSMENT

**Name:** _____     **Date:** _____

You have learned a lot of information about crabs and turtles this week. Suppose you were chosen to explain about crabs and turtles to third graders. You would need to explain how crabs and turtles live and grow. What is a crab? What is a turtle? What are their important characteristics? You would also need to explain how crabs and turtles live and survive in the their habitats.

A.  DRAW A PICTURE TO SHOW HOW CRABS AND TURTLES LIVE AND GROW. Be sure to label all the important parts.

B. Using your drawing and what you can remember about what you have learned this week, WRITE AN EXPLANATION OF HOW CRABS AND TURTLES LIVE AND GROW. How are they similar? How are they different from each other? Be sure to write about their important characteristics. Think about how crabs and turtles live and survive in their habitat. Use science ideas in your explanation. Write as much as you can.

_____
_____
_____
_____
_____
_____
_____
_____
_____
_____
_____
_____
_____
_____
_____
_____
_____
_____
_____
_____
_____
_____
_____
_____
_____
_____
_____

# RUBRIC FOR CODING THE PERFORMANCE ASSESSMENT OF PRIOR-KNOWLEDGE, DRAWING, AND WRITING

This rubric is the same for the prior-knowledge, drawing, and writing (conceptual knowledge) portions of the performance assessment. Levels can also be converted to letter grades.

## Level 1

At this level the students present: (1) no information; (2) scientifically inaccurate information; (3) one appropriately identified feature, structure, or function for each animal; or (4) two features, structures, or functions for only one animal.

## Level 2

Students present a combination of two to four general or specific features of the animals or structures of functions for at least one of the animals. However, no relationships among them are demonstrated. At this level students may also present scientifically inaccurate information.

## Level 3

At this level the student may present accurate and relevant information for a minimum of four specific features, structures, or functions of one animal. An alternative response is that students could present any relationships or connections among the structures, features, and the functions of the animals, but the relationships are left implicit through vague comparisons, meaning that they don't explain "why." No explanations for the relationships among features or structures are presented.

## Level 4

At this level a student presents all of the necessary elements for a Level 3, but the relationships or connections among features, structures, or functions of the animals are presented explicitly. Students at this level explain "why." However, these relationships are stated only for one animal, and those for the other animal remain implicit or vague. Students may also present their answers in the form of a clear relationship for one animal that was not transferable to the other. Explanations are explicitly included and are distinguishable from particular facts or statements about the animal and structural or functional characteristics.

## Level 5

At this level students write about the explicit relationships among features, structures, and/or functions of both animals. The comparison is often parallel, with one type of structural characteristic of one of the animals comparable to a type of structural characteristic of the other animal, demonstrating symmetry. However, answers at this level lack connections among the relationships among the features, structures, or functions. An alternative means for obtaining a Level 5 is to present a fully explained, systemic (Level 6) response for only one animal, with very limited information on the second animal.

## Level 6

At this level students clearly and fully explicate the principles that link the features of the animals in terms of "systems." A systemic answer is given for both animals. For example, life cycles or animal characteristics of certain structures and the relationships among these features, structures, and functions of the respective species are stated. The systems are governed by principles centered around the characteristics of the species, such as habitat, survival, growth and life cycles, food chains, adaptations, and so on. (Note: When students have a lot of prior knowledge on a topic, the rubric may have to be extended to Level 9 to allow for this level of knowledge. If students do not have much prior knowledge, use the rubric to Level 6.)

## Level 7

Students provide a Level 6 answer plus elaborated features for both animals.

## Level 8

Students provide a Level 7 answer plus elaborated relationships among the features and functions of both animals.

## Level 9

Students provide a Level 8 answer plus an elaboration of the systems for both animals.

# APPENDIX C

## Margaret's Weather Book List

| Book Title | Author(s) |
|---|---|
| *Amy Loves the Wind* | Julia Hoban |
| *Animals in Winter* | Henrietta Brancroft & Richard G. VanGelder |
| *The Big Snow* | Berta Hader & Elmer Hader |
| *Brave Irene* | William Steig |
| *Can It Rain Cats and Dogs?* | Melvin Berger & Gilda Berger |
| *City Storm* | Mary Parker |
| *The Cloud Book* | Tomie de Paola |
| *Cloud Dance* | Thomas Locker |
| *Cloudy with a Chance of Meatballs* | Judith Barrett |
| *The Day It Rained Forever* | Virginia Gross |
| *Dear Rebecca, Winter Is Here* | Jean Craighead George |
| *Do Tornadoes Really Twist?* | Melvin Berger & Gilda Berger |
| *Down Comes the Rain* | Franklyn Mansfield Branley |
| *A Drop of Water* | Walter Wick |
| *Fantastic Facts: Weather* | Robin Kerrod |
| *Feel the Wind* | Arthur Dorros |
| *First Field Guide to Weather* | Jonathan D. Kahl, Audobon Society |
| *Flash Crash Rumble Roll* | Franklyn Mansfield Branley |
| *How the Weather Works* | Reader's Digest |
| *Hurricane* | David Wiesner |
| *Hurricanes* | Weather Channel |
| *Hurricanes and Tornadoes* | Neil Morris |
| *Icebergs and Glaciers* | Seymour Simon |
| *The Jacket I Wear in the Snow* | Shirley Neitzel |
| *The Kids Book of Weather Forecasting* | Mark Breen |
| *The Kingfisher Science Encyclopedia* | Charles Taylor (Editor) |
| *The Kingfisher Young People's Book of Planet Earth* | Martin Tedfern |
| *Lightning* | Seymour Simon |
| *Lightning and Thunderstorms* | The Weather Channel |
| *A Little Bit of Winter* | Paul Stewart |
| *Magic School Bus inside a Hurricane* | Joanna Cole |
| *My Spring Robin* | Anne F. Rockwell |

| | |
|---|---|
| *On the Same Day in March: A Tour of the World's Weather* | Marilyn Singer |
| *Pink Snow and Other Weird Weather* | Jennifer Dussling |
| *Questions and Answers about Weather* | M. Jean Craig |
| *Rain Player* | David Wisniewski |
| *The Reasons for Seasons* | Gail Gibbons |
| *Snip, Snip, Snow* | Nancy Poydar |
| *Snow* | Uri Shulevitz |
| *Snow Child* | Jody J. Davidson |
| *Snow Pumpkin* | Carole Lexa Schaefer |
| *The Snow Walker* | Margaret & Charles Wetterer |
| *Snowballs* | Lois Ehlert |
| *Snowflake Bentley* | Jacqueline Briggs Martin |
| *Storm Chasers* | Gail Herman |
| *Stranger in the Woods* | Carl R. Sams & Jean Stoick |
| *Sunshine Makes the Season* | Franklyn Mansfield Branley |
| *Tornado Alert* | Franklyn Mansfield Branley |
| *Tornadoes* | Seymour Simon |
| *Tornadoes* | Weather Channel |
| *Twisters* | Lucille Recht Penner |
| *Wacky Weather* | Annalisa McMorrow |
| *Water, Water Everywhere* | Melvin Berger & Gilda Berger |
| *Weather* | Eyewitness Books |
| *Weather* | Eyewitness Explorers |
| *Weather* | Nature Company |
| *Weather* | Seymour Simon |
| *Weather Forecasting* | Gail Gibbons |
| *Weather Poems for All Seasons* | Lee Bennett Hopkins |
| *Weather Words and What They Mean* | Gail Gibbons |
| *Weather and Sky* | Discovery Channel |
| *What Will the Weather Be?* | Lynda DeWitt |
| *What Will the Weather Be: Animal Signs* | Hubert J. Davis |
| *What Will the Weather Be Like Today?* | Paul Rodgers |
| *What's the Big Idea, Ben Franklin?* | Jean Fritz |
| *What's the Weather Like Today?* | Rozanne Lanczak Williams |
| *When Autumn Comes* | Robert Maass |
| *When Spring Comes* | Robert Maass |
| *When Summer Comes* | Robert Maass |
| *When a Storm Comes Up* | Allan Fowler |
| *When It Starts to Snow* | Phyllis Gershator |
| *Why Do Leaves Change Color?* | Betsy C. Maestro |
| *Wild Weather: Floods!* | Lorraine Jean Hopping |
| *Wild Weather: Tornadoes!* | Lorraine Jean Hopping |
| *The Wind Blew* | Pat Hutchins |
| *Winter Days in the Big Woods* | Laura Ingalls Wilder |
| *Winter on the Farm* | Laura Ingalls Wilder |

# APPENDIX D

## Self-Monitoring Checklist for Reports

Name: _____  Date: _____  Topic: _____

|  | Yes | No |
|---|---|---|
| I have found enough information to answer my question about my topic | ____ | ____ |
| I have found information from at least three sources on my topic | ____ | ____ |
| I have written my notes on index cards | ____ | ____ |
| I have organized my cards to make sense | ____ | ____ |
| I have written my draft from my cards | ____ | ____ |
| I used clear and complete sentences when writing my report | ____ | ____ |
| I am have edited and revised my draft | ____ | ____ |
| I have presented my report orally | ____ | ____ |

### SCORING RUBRIC

7–8 out of 8 are checked—report is excellent

5–7 out of 8 are checked—report is satisfactory

Fewer than 5 are checked—report needs improvement

# APPENDIX E

## Motivations for Reading Questionnaire* (MRQ)

| | 1<br>Not at<br>all like<br>me | 2<br>Some-<br>what<br>like<br>me | 3<br>More<br>like<br>me | 4<br>Most<br>like<br>me |
|---|---|---|---|---|

**Intrinsic Motivations:**

*Reading Efficacy*

I know I will do well in reading this year.

I am a good reader.

I learn more from reading than most students in the class.

In comparison to my other school subjects, I am best at reading.

*Challenge*

I like hard, challenging books.

I like it when the questions in books make me think.

I usually learn difficult things by reading.

If the project is interesting, I can read difficult material.

If a book is interesting, I don't care how hard it is to read.

*Curiosity*

If the teacher discusses something interesting, I might read more about it.

I read about my hobbies to learn more about them.

I read to learn new information about topics that interest me.

I like to read about new things.

*Revised Version.* To administer this questionnaire, the statements need to be presented in random order (without the categories or headings) and numbered. The students write the numeral (1, 2, 3, or 4) next to each statement that ranks how true the statement is for them.

148

| | 1<br>Not at<br>all like<br>me | 2<br>Some-<br>what<br>like<br>me | 3<br>More<br>like<br>me | 4<br>Most<br>like<br>me |
|---|---|---|---|---|

If I am reading about an interesting topic, I sometimes lose track of time. _____ _____ _____ _____

I enjoy reading books about people in different countries. _____ _____ _____ _____

*Involvement*

I read stories about fantasy and make believe. _____ _____ _____ _____

I make pictures in my mind when I read. _____ _____ _____ _____

I feel like I make friends with people in good books. _____ _____ _____ _____

I like mysteries. _____ _____ _____ _____

I enjoy a long, involved story or fiction book. _____ _____ _____ _____

I read a lot of adventure stories. _____ _____ _____ _____

*Importance*

It is very important to me to be a good reader. _____ _____ _____ _____

In comparison to other activities I do, it is very important to me to be a good reader. _____ _____ _____ _____

**Extrinsic Motivations:**

*Recognition*

My friends sometimes tell me I am a good reader. _____ _____ _____ _____

I like hearing the teacher say I read well. _____ _____ _____ _____

I am happy when someone recognizes my reading. _____ _____ _____ _____

My parents often tell me what a good job I am doing in reading. _____ _____ _____ _____

I like to get compliments for my reading. _____ _____ _____ _____

*Grades*

I look forward to finding out my reading grade. _____ _____ _____ _____

Grades are a good way to see how well you are doing in reading. _____ _____ _____ _____

I read to improve my grades. _____ _____ _____ _____

My parents ask me about my reading grade. _____ _____ _____ _____

*Social*

I visit the library often with my family. _____ _____ _____ _____

I often read to my brother or my sister. _____ _____ _____ _____

I sometimes read to my parents. _____ _____ _____ _____

My friends and I like to trade things to read. _____ _____ _____ _____

I talk to my friends about what I am reading. _____ _____ _____ _____

I like to help my friends with their schoolwork in reading. _____ _____ _____ _____

I like to tell my family about what I am reading. _____ _____ _____ _____

|  | 1<br>Not at<br>all like<br>me | 2<br>Some-<br>what<br>like<br>me | 3<br>More<br>like<br>me | 4<br>Most<br>like<br>me |
|---|---|---|---|---|

*Competition*

I like being the only one who knows an answer in something we read.

I like being the best at reading.

It is important for me to see my name on a list of good readers.

I try to get more answers right than my friends.

I like to finish my reading before other students.

I am willing to work hard to read better than my friends.

*Compliance*

I do as little schoolwork as possible in reading.

I read because I have to.

I always do my reading work exactly as the teacher wants it.

Finishing every reading assignment is very important to me.

I always try to finish my reading on time.

*Reading Work Avoidance*

I don't like to read out loud in class.

I don't like having to write about what I read.

I don't like reading stories that are too short.

I don't like reading something when the words are too difficult.

I don't like vocabulary questions.

I don't like it when there are too many people in the story.

# References

Alexander, P. A., & Judy, J. A. (1988). The interaction of domain-specific and strategic knowledge in academic performance. *Review of Educational Research, 58,* 375–404.

Alexander, P. A., Kulikowich, J. M., & Jetton, T. L. (1994). The role of subject matter knowledge and interest in the processing of linear and nonlinear texts. *Review of Educational Research, 64*(2), 201–252.

Alexander, P. A., Schallert, D. L., & Hare, V. C. (1991). Coming to terms: How researchers in learning and literacy talk about knowledge. *Review of Educational Research, 61,* 315–343.

Almasi, J. F. (1996). The nature of fourth graders' sociocognitive conflicts in peer-led and teacher-led discussion of literature. *Reading Research Quarterly, 30,* 314–351.

Ames, C. (1992a). Achievement goals and the classroom motivational climate. In D. H. Schunk & J. L. Meece (Eds.), *Student perceptions in the classroom* (pp. 327–348). Hillsdale, NJ: Erlbaum.

Anderson, E. (1998). *Motivational and cognitive influences on conceptual knowledge acquisition: The combination of science observations and interesting texts.* Unpublished doctoral dissertation, University of Maryland, College Park.

Anderson, E., & Guthrie, J. T. (1997, April). *Influences of two components of search and instruction on conceptual learning.* Paper presented at the annual meeting of the American Education Research Association, Chicago.

Anderson, R. C., & Pearson, P. D. (1984). A schema-theoretic view of basic processes in reading comprehension. In P. D. Pearson (Ed.), *Handbook of reading research* (pp. 225–291). New York: Longman.

Anderson, R. C., Heibert, E. H., Scott, J. A., & Wilkinson, I. A. (1985). *Becoming a nation of readers: The report of the commission of reading.* Washington, DC: National Institute of Education.

Armbruster, B. B., & Armstrong, J. O. (1993). Locating information in text: A focus on children in the elementary grades. *Contemporary Educational Psychology, 18,* 139–161.

Armbruster, B. B., & Gudbrandsen, B. (1986). Reading comprehension instruction in social studies programs. *Reading Research Quarterly, 21,* 36–48.

Asher, S. R. (1980). Topic interest and children's reading comprehension. In R. J. Spiro, B. C. Bruce, & W. F. Brewer (Eds.), *Theoretical issues in reading comprehension* (pp. 525–534). Hillsdale, NJ: Erlbaum.

Baldwin, R. S., Peleg-Bruckner, Z., & McClintock, A. H. (1985). Effects of topic interest and prior knowledge on reading comprehension. *Reading Research Quarterly, 20,* 497–504.

Bandura, A. (1986). *Social foundations of thought and action: A social cognitive theory.* Englewood Cliffs, NJ: Prentice-Hall.

Bandura, A. (1993). Perceived self-efficacy in cognitive development and functioning. *Educational Psychologist, 28,* 117–148.

Baumann, J., Hoffman, J., Moon, J., & Duffy-Hester, A. M. (1998). Where are teachers' voices in the phonics/whole language debate? Results from a survey of U.S. elementary teachers. *The Reading Teacher, 51,* 385–414.

Block, C. C., & Pressley, M. (Eds.). (2001). *Comprehension instruction: Research-based best practices.* New York: Guilford Press.

Brophy, J. (1981). Teacher praise: A functional analysis. *Review of Educational Research, 51,* 5–32.

Brophy, J.(1983). Conceptualizing student motivation. *Educational Psychologist, 18,* 200– 215.

Brown, A. L. (1992). Design experiments: Theoretical and methodological challenges in creating complex interventions in classroom settings. *Journal of the Learning Sciences, 2,* 141–178.

Brown, A. L., Bransford, J. D., Ferrara, R. A., & Campione, J. S. (1983). Learning, remembering and understanding. In H. Flavell & E. H. Markman (Eds.), *Handbook of child psychology: Cognitive development* (Vol. 3, pp. 177–266). New York: Wiley.

Calkins, L. (1997). *Raising lifelong learners: A parent's guide.* Reading, MA: Addison-Wesley.

Chi, M. T. H., DeLeeuw, N., Chiu, M., & LaVancher, C. (1994). Eliciting self-explanations improves understanding. *Cognitive Science, 18,* 439–477.

Christianson, S. A. (Ed.). (1992). *The handbook of emotion and memory: Research and theory.* Hillsdale, NJ: Erlbaum.

Craig, F. I. M., & Lockhart, R. S. (1972). Levels of processing: A framework for memory research. *Journal of Verbal Learning and Verbal Behavior, 11,* 671–684.

Csikszentmihalyi, M. (1988). The flow experience and its significance for human psychology. In M. Csikszentmihalyi & I. S. Csikszentmihalyi (Eds.), *Optimal experience: Psychological studies of flow in consciousness* (pp. 15–35). Cambridge, MA: Cambridge University Press.

Deci, E. L., & Ryan, R. M. (1985). *Intrinsic motivation and self-determination in human behavior.* New York: Plenum Press.

Deci, E. L., Schwartz, A. J., Scheiman, L., & Ryan, R. M. (1981). An instrument to assess adults' orientations toward control versus autonomy with children: Reflections on intrinsic motivation and perceived competence. *Journal of Educational Psychology, 73*(5), 642–650.

Deci, E. L., Vallerand, R. J., Pelletier, L. G., & Ryan, R. M. (1991). Motivation and education: The self-determination perspective. *Educational Psychologist, 26,* 325–346.

Denner, P. R., & Rickards, J. P. (1987). A developmental comparison of the effects of provided and generated questions on text recall. *Contemporary Educational Psychology, 12,* 135–146.

Dole, J. A., Duffy, G. G., Roehler, L. R., & Pearson, P. D. (1991). Moving from the old to the new: Research on reading comprehension instruction. *Review of Educational Research, 61,* 239–264.

Dreher, M. J., & Guthrie, J. T. (1990). Cognitive processes in textbook chapter search tasks. *Reading Research Quarterly, 25,* 323–339.

Eccles, J. S., Wigfield, A., Midgley, C., Reuman, D., MacIver, D., & Feldlaufer, H. (1993). Negative effects of traditional middle schools on students' motivation. *The Elementary School Journal, 93*(5), 553–574.

Entin, E. B., & Klare, G. R. (1985). Relationships of measures of interest, prior knowledge, and readability to comprehension of expository passages. *Advances in Reading/Language Research, 3,* 9–38.

Flink, C., Boggianno, A. K., Main, D. S., Barrett, M., & Katz, P. A. (1992). Children's achievement-related behaviors: The role of extrinsic and intrinsic motivational orientations. In A. K. Boggiano & T. S. Pittman (Eds.), *Achievement and motivation: A socio-developmental perspective* (pp. 189–214). New York: Cambridge University Press.

Gambrell, L. B. (1996, May). Creating classroom cultures that foster reading motivation. *The Reading Teacher, 50,* 14–25.

Gambrell, L. B., & Marinak, B. (1997). Incentives and intrinsic motivation to read. In J. T. Guthrie & A. Wigfield (Eds.), *Reading engagement: Motivating readers through integrated instruction* (pp. 205–217). Newark, DE: International Reading Association.

Glynn, S. M. (1994). *Teaching science with analogies: A strategy for teachers and textbook authors* (Reading Research Report No. 15). Athens, GA: Universities of Georgia and Maryland, National Reading Research Center.

Glynn, S. M., & Duit, R. (Eds.). (1995). *Learning science in the schools: Research reforming practice.* Mahwah, NJ: Erlbaum.

Goodlad, J. I. (1984). *A place called school.* New York: McGraw-Hill.

Grolnick, W. S., & Ryan, R. M. (1987). Autonomy in children's learning: An experimental and individual difference investigation. *Journal of Personality and Social Psychology, 52*, 273–288.

Guthrie, J. T., & Alao, S. (1997). Designing contexts to increase motivations for reading. *Educational Psychologist, 32*, 95–107.

Guthrie, J. T., & Anderson, E. (1999). Engagement in reading: Processes of motivated, strategic, knowledgeable, social readers. In J. T. Guthrie & D. E. Alvermann (Eds.), *Engaged reading: Processes, practices, and policy implications* (pp. 17–45). New York: Teachers College Press.

Guthrie, J. T., Anderson, E., Alao, S., & Rinehart, J. M. (1999). Influences of Concept-Oriented Reading Instruction on strategy use and conceptual learning from text. *Elementary School Journal, 99*(4), 343–366.

Guthrie, J. T., Britten, T., & Barker, K. G. (1991). Roles of document structure, cognitive strategy, and awareness in searching for information. *Reading Research Quarterly, 26*, 300–324.

Guthrie, J. T., & Cox, K. (1998). Portrait of an engaging classroom: Principles of Concept-Oriented Reading Instruction for diverse students. In K. Harris (Ed.), *Teaching every child every day: Learning in diverse schools and classrooms* (pp. 77–131). Cambridge, MA: Brookline Books.

Guthrie, J. T., Cox, K., Anderson, E., Harris, K., Mazzoni, S., & Rach, L. (1998). Principles of integrated instruction for engagement in reading. *Educational Psychology Review, 10*, 177–199.

Guthrie, J. T., Cox, K. E., Knowles, K. T., Buehl, M., Mazzoni, S. A., & Fasulo, L. (2000). Building toward coherent instruction. In L. Baker, M. J. Dreher, & J. T. Guthrie (Eds.), *Engaging young readers: Promoting achievement and motivation* (pp.209–236). New York: Guilford Press.

Guthrie, J. T., & McCann, A. D., (1996). Idea circles: Peer collaborations for conceptual learning. In L. B. Gambrell & J. F. Almasi (Eds.), *Lively Discussions!: Fostering engaged reading.* Newark, DE: International Reading Association.

Guthrie, J. T., & McCann, A. D. (1997). Characteristics of classrooms that promote motivations and strategies for learning. In J. T. Guthrie & A. Wigfield (Eds.), *Reading engagement: motivating readers through integrated instruction* (pp. 128–148). Newark, DE: International Reading Association.

Guthrie, J. T., Schafer, W., & Hutchinson, S. R. (1991). Relations of document literacy and prose literacy to occupational and societal characteristics of young black and white adults. *Reading Research Quarterly, 26*, 30–48.

Guthrie, J. T., Schafer, W. D., Wang, Y. Y., & Afflerbach, P. (1995). Relationships of instruction of reading: An exploration of social, cognitive, and instructional connections. *Reading Research Quarterly, 30*, 8–25.

Guthrie, J. T., Van Meter, P., Hancock, G. R., McCann, A., Anderson, E., & Alao, S. (1998). Does Concept-Oriented Reading Instruction increase strategy-use and conceptual learning from text? *Journal of Educational Psychology, 90*, 261–278.

Guthrie, J. T., Van Meter, P., McCann, A. D., Wigfield, A., Bennett, L., Poundstone, C. C., Rice, M. E., Fabisch, F. M., Hunt, B., & Mitchell, A. M. (1996). Growth of literacy engagement: Changes in motivations and strategies during Concept-Oriented Reading Instruction. *Reading Research Quarterly, 31*, 306–322.

Guthrie, J. T., Weber, S., & Kimmerly, N. (1993). Searching documents: Cognitive processes and deficits in understanding graphs, tables, and illustrations. *Contemporary Educational Psychology, 18*, 186–221.

Harvey, S. (1998). *Nonfiction matters: Reading, writing, and research in grades 3–8*. York, ME: Stenhouse.

Harvey, S., & Goudvis, A. (2000). *Strategies that work: Teaching comprehension to enhance understanding*. York, ME: Stenhouse.

Hidi, S. (1990). Interest and its contribution as a mental resource for learning. *Review of Educational Research, 60*, 549–571.

Keene, E. O., & Zimmerman, S. (1997). *Mosaic of thought: Teaching comprehension in a reader's workshop*. Portsmouth, NH: Heinemann.

King, A. (1994). Autonomy and question asking: The role of personal control in guided student-generated questioning. *Learning and Individual Differences, 6*, 163–185.

Kintsch, W. (1986). Learning from text. *Cognition and Instruction, 3*, 87–108.

Kintsch, W. (1988). The role of knowledge in discourse comprehension: A construction-integration model. *Psychological Review, 95*, 163–182.

Kohn, A. (1993). *Punished by rewards: The trouble with gold stars, incentive plans, A's, praise, and other bribes*. Boston: Houghton Mifflin.

Leipzig, D. H., & Afflerbach, P. (2000). Determining the suitability of assessments: Using the CURRV framework. In L. Baker, M. J. Dreher, & J. T. Guthrie (Eds.), *Engaging young readers: Promoting achievement and motivation* (pp. 159–187). New York: Guilford Press.

McLyod, V. (1979). The effects on extrinsic rewards of differential value on high and low intrinsic interest. *Child Development, 50*, 1010–1019.

Meece, J. L., Blumenfeld, P. C., & Hoyle, R. H. (1988). Students' goal orientations and cognitive engagement in classroom activities. *Journal of Educational Psychology, 80*(4), 515–523.

Meece, J. L., & Miller, S. D. (1999). Changes in elementary school children's achievement goals for reading and writing: Results of a longitudinal and an intervention study. *Scientific Studies of Reading, 3*(3), 207–230.

Moore, S. A., & Fawson, P. C. (1992, December). *Reading incentive programs: beliefs and practices*. Paper presented at the 42nd Annual Meeting of the National Reading Conference, San Antonio, TX.

Morrow, L. M. (1992). The impact of a literature-based program on literacy achievement, use of literature and attitudes of children from minority backgrounds. *Reading Research Quarterly, 27*, 250–275.

Mosenthal, P. B. (1985). Defining the expository discourse continuum: Towards a taxonomy of expository text types. *Poetics, 14*, 387–414.

Mosenthal, P. B. (1987). The goals of reading research and practice: Making sense of the many theories of reading. *The Reading Teacher, 40*, 694–698.

Nolen, S. B., & Nichols, J. G. (1994). A place to begin (again) in research on student motivation: Teachers' beliefs. *Teaching and Teacher Education, 10*, 57–69.

O'Flahavan, J. F. (1989). *An exploration of the effects of participant structure upon literacy development in reading group discussion*. Unpublished doctoral dissertation, University of Illinois, Urbana-Champaign.

Ogle, D. (1986). K–W–L: A teaching model that develops active reading in expository text. *The Reading Teacher, 39*, 563–570.

Oldfather, P., & Dahl, K. (1994). Toward a social constructivist reconceptualization of intrinsic motivation for literacy learning. *Journal of Reading Behavior, 26*, 139–158.

Oldfather, P., & McLaughlin, J. (1993). Gaining and losing voice: A longitudinal study of students' continuing impulse to learn across elementary and middle school contexts. *Research in Middle Level Education, 17*, 1–25.

Pearson, P. D., Dole, J. A., Duffy, G. G., & Roehler, L. R. (1992). Developing expertise in reading comprehension: What should be taught and how should it be taught? In J. Farstrup & S. J. Samuels (Eds.), *What research has to say to the teacher of reading* (2nd ed., pp. 145–167). Newark, DE: International Reading Association.

Pintrich, P. R., & DeGroot, E. V. (1990). Motivational and self-regulated learning components of classroom academic performance. *Journal of Educational Psychology, 82*, 33–40.

Pressley, M., Rankin, J., & Yokoi, L. (1996). A survey of instructional practices of primary teachers nominated as effective in promoting literacy. *Elementary School Journal, 96*(4), 363–383.

Renninger, K. A. (1988). *Effects of interest and non-interest on student performance with tasks of mathematical word problems and reading comprehension.* Paper presented at the annual meeting of the American Educational Research Association, New Orleans, LA.

Rumelhart, D. E. (1980). Schemata: The building blocks of cognition. In R. J. Spiro, B. C. Bruce, & W. F. Brewer (Eds.), *Theoretical issues in reading comprehension* (pp. 35–58). Hillsdale, NJ: Erlbaum.

Schiefele, U. (1992). Topic interest and levels of text comprehension. In K. A. Renninger, S. Hidi, & A. Krapp (Eds.), *The role of interest in learning and development* (pp. 151–182). Hillsdale, NJ: Erlbaum.

Sheiefele, U. (1996). Topic interest, text representation, and quality of experience. *Contemporary Educational Psychology, 21*, 3–18.

Schiefele, U., & Krapp, A. (1996). Topic interest and free recall of expository text. *Learning and Individual Differences, 8*, 141–160.

Schraw, G., Bruning, R., & Svoboda, C. (1995). Source of situational interest. *Journal of Reading Behavior, 27*, 1–17.

Schunk, D. H. (1984). Enhancing self-efficacy and achievment through rewards and goals: Motivational and informational effects. *Journal of Educational Research, 78*(1), 29–34.

Skinner, E. A., & Belmont, M. J. (1993). Motivation in the classroom: Reciprocal feedback during reading teacher behavior and student engagement across the school year. *Journal of Educational Psychology, 85*, 571–581.

Skinner, E. A., Wellborn, J. G., & Connell, J. P. (1990). What it takes to do well in school and whether I've got it: A process model of perceived control and children's engagement and achievement in school. *Journal of Eduational Psychology, 82*(1), 22–32.

Slavin, R. (1990). *Cooperative learning: Theory, research, and practice.* Englewood Cliffs, NJ: Prentice Hall.

Stanovich, K. E., & Cunningham, A. E. (1993). Where does knowledge come from? Specific associations between print exposure and information acquisition. *Journal of Educational Psychology, 85*, 211–229.

Stipek, D. (1996). Motivation and instruction. In D. C. Berliner & R. C. Calfee (Eds.), *Handbook of educational psychology* (pp. 85–113). New York: Simon & Schuster/Macmillan.

Stipek, D., & Seal, K. (2001). *Motivated minds: Raising children to love learning.* New York: Holt.

Sweet, A., Guthrie, J. T., & Ng, M. (1998). Teachers' perceptions and students reading motivations. *Journal of Educational Psychology, 90*(2), 210–223.

Thayer, R. E. (1989). *The biopsychology of mood and arousal.* New York: Oxford University Press.

Tovani, C. (2000). *I read it but I don't get it: Comprehension strategies for adolescent readers.* Portland, ME: Stenhouse.

Turner, J. C. (1995). The influence of classroom contexts on young children's motivation for literacy. *Reading Research Quarterly, 30*, 410–441.

van Dijk, T. A., & Kintsch, W. (1983). *Strategies of discourse comprehension.* Orlando, FL: Academic Press.

Vygotsky, L. S. (1978). *Mind in society.* Cambridge, MA: Harvard University Press.

Wade, S. E. (1992). How interest affects learning from text. In K. A. Renninger, S. Hidi, & A. Krapp (Eds.), *The role of interest in learning and development* (pp. 255–277). Hillsdale, NJ: Erlbaum.

Wentzel, K. R. (1996). Social and academic motivation in middle school: Concurrent and long-term relations to academic effort. *Journal of Early Adolescence, 16*, 390–406.

Wigfield, A.(1997). Children's motivations for reading and reading engagement. In J. T. Guthrie

& A. Wigfield (Eds.), *Reading engagment: Motivating readers through integrated instruction* (pp.14–33). Newark, DE: International Reading Association.

Wigfield, A., & Guthrie, J. T. (1997). Relations of children's motivation for reading to the amount and breadth of their reading. *Journal of Educational Psychology, 89,* 420–432.

Wigfield, A., Guthrie, J. T., & McGough, K. (1996). *A questionnaire measure of children's motivations for reading* (Instructional Resource No. 22). Athens, GA: National Reading Research Center.

Williamson, R. A. (1996). Self-questioning: An aid to metacognition. *Reading Horizons, 37,* 31–47.

Wlodkowski, R. (1985). *Enhancing adult motivation to learn.* San Francisco: Jossey-Bass.

Wong, B. (1985). Self-questioning instructional research: A review. *Review of Educational Research, 55,* 227–268.

Worthy, J. (2000). Teachers' and students' suggestions for motivating middle school students to read. *Yearbook of the National Reading Conference, 49,* 441–451.

Worthy, J. (2002). The intermediate grades: What makes intermediate-grade students want to read? *The Reading Teacher, 55*(6), 568–569.

# Index